MW01075418

I AM
in-di-vid-u-al
One person, task, or action
Acting alone for the benefit of "I" and/or "We"

WE ARE
In-di-vid-u-al
Many individuals, tasks, or actions
Acting together as ONE for the benefit of "We" and/or "I"

I HAVE
in-flu-ence
My greatest responsibility is
how I affect others with all I do or say.

What people are saying about *Positive Influence: Be the "I" in Team*

"*Positive Influence: Be the 'I' in Team* is a toolbox for managers to understand how their personal influence can affect every level of Maslow's Hierarchy of Needs."

—Kirk Allen, President & CEO, Sloan Global Holdings

"Understanding the value of our influence can be a challenge for many. My influence has been to help people communicate and connect more effectively through *The Fine Art of Small Talk. Positive Influence: Be the 'I' in Team* is an important book that will enhance our understanding of influence in a positive and encouraging way."

—Debra Fine, author of *The Fine Art of Small Talk*

"Leaders have paid lip service to the value of their team members for too long while not exhibiting the behaviors that reflect a true commitment — and they are paying the price. In the timely and thought-provoking *Positive Influence: Be the 'I' in Team*, Smith and Griffin bring the broad subject of influence to the ground level and show leaders what effective behaviors, mindset, and action look like in the real world. A timely and relevant leadership guide during turbulent times. Grab a highlighter and write all over this book."

— David Avrin, author of *Why Customers Leave and How to Win Them Back*

"Positive Influence is another great addition to The "I" in Team Series. I enjoyed the vulnerability shared by the author with personal case studies that I can relate to"

—Brian Brogen, Founding Author of the Voices For Leadership Series

"I love how Brian & Mary highlight choices and influence we have in our lives to make a positive impact to inspire people around us. I encourage your entire team to read this book."

—Rusty Komori, Author, Beyond The Lines & Beyond The Game

This book should be gifted to all college graduates entering the workforce. We would all be so lucky to hire someone who has taken the time to absorb Brian and Mary's discerning advice.

—Audrey Grunst, LCSW, Therapist & Founder of Simply Bee

Positive Influence

Be the "I" in Team

Brian Smith PhD and Mary Griffin

Made for Success Publishing
P.O. Box 1775, Issaquah, WA 98027
www.MadeForSuccess.com

Distributed by Made for Success Publishing

First Printing

Library of Congress Cataloging-in-Publication data
Smith, Brian and Griffin, Mary
POSITIVE INFLUENCE: Be the "I" in Team

p. cm.

LCCN: 2022921765
ISBN: 978-1-64146-762-9 *(Hardback)*
ISBN: 978-1-64146-763-6 *(eBook)*
ISBN: 978-1-64146-764-3 *(Audiobook)*

Printed in the United States of America

For further information contact Made for Success Publishing
+1(425)526-6480 or email service@madeforsuccess.net

Table of Contents

Acknowledgements

It would be nearly impossible to thank all of those who have had an influence on me. People I have never even met, and never will get the chance to meet, have influenced my life. I believe in the effect we have on the lives of the people we touch. Their memory of us, the impact we had on them, remains until they pass from this life. This is one reason I believe our influence is the single greatest responsibility we have as human beings.

That said, we all have a number of individuals who impact us in such a way that they leave a lasting influence and lifelong memories, and I have many of those individuals in my life. First, there are my parents—all of them. My biological mother and father created a foundation for me that influences who I am. My stepparents, Bill, Michele, and Jeff, have all brought me lessons and joy that continue to influence me on a daily basis.

Leonard Rice and Kevin Chwala are nearly lifelong friends. Leonard has been a true friend to me since the early 1990s, and his friendship has been nothing but a ray of sunshine in my memories. Kevin and I have known each other since third grade. He's like a brother to me. Another friend and trusted member of my team, Braden Zoet, has been pivotal in bringing the ideas in the *"I" in Team* series to life. His thorough approach to all of life is an inspiration to me.

My family—René, Kristin, Mary, and Henry—have all positively influenced my life. Henry, my son, brings me so much joy and pride, and the person he has become continues to amaze me. Kristin, my daughter, is a great source of pride for me as well, as are her daughter, Kenzi, and her husband, Isaiah. I look forward to watching them grow as individuals and as a family. Mary, my other daughter and co-author, is one of the most amazing humans on the planet. She and her husband, Spencer, bring me so much joy whenever we are together. With Mary, I learn, teach, and share life in a way so that I never question what we do or why we do it, not even for a moment.

Finally, my beautiful wife, René, has been my life partner since 1990. She is the rock of our entire family and the catalyst for us all to be amazing. René's energy and approach to life has influenced not only us but everyone she interacts with to be better and spread positivity. René's energy is infectious.

I want to thank and acknowledge all the people who have made me who I am today and who made this series possible. Your influence has positively affected me for the remainder of my days.

Foreword

by René Smith

I met Brian 30 years ago while working at an auto repair shop. He was my boss, and eventually, he fired me! In all honesty, it was justified as I was a flaky 20-year-old kid who would rather goof off than go to work. What makes the story even better is that after he fired me, he asked me out on a date—and the rest, as they say, is history!

When Brian told me he and our daughter, Mary, were writing a second book, I was honored that he asked me to write the foreword. So, here I am, hoping to impart a bit of wisdom on what influence means to me. And here you are, hoping to glean a bit of knowledge about how your individual influence can benefit yourself and those around you. The advice I have for you as you begin this journey takes us back to when I was first pregnant.

I wanted to tackle parenting with a different philosophy than the one my parents had. Therefore, I spent both of my pregnancies reading parenting and self-help books. I stored in my memory what I felt was important, what *spoke* to me, and left the rest. One lesson that stood out—that some of you may already know—is to count to 10 when you are feeling emotional. Of course, this advice is great, in theory, but can be a tough thing to do in the heat of the moment. Additionally, another lesson that stuck with me was to imagine that there was a camera recording my actions for a pretend audience. The advice was, "Would you, then, be proud of your actions in front of that audience?"

For me, pretending I had a fake audience worked better than counting to 10. As a parent, it wasn't always a fake audience. My children were always with and watching me, learning from me, as all children do. However, this trick helped me so much that I began to use it in my everyday activities. I would ask myself, "Would my pretend audience like that I let the person at the grocery store—with only four items in their cart—go ahead of me when I had a full cart? Would my pretend audience like to hear me keep my cool while dealing with a difficult phone call?" This trick helped me slow down and think, *Am I proud of how I am using my influence right now?*

If I felt good about the film I was producing, then I felt like I was on the right track. There was also an added benefit to my filmmaking: I felt really good about myself! I realized I was becoming a better parent and a better person. Ultimately, I felt like I was having a better influence on those around me. Then, on the other hand, if upon reviewing my film I saw that there was room for improvement, I tried to learn from it and push myself to be better next time. While I knew that my audience was "pretend" most of the time, I also had my children to think about. Then, I considered, "Is my audience really 'pretend?'"

It may look like people are in their own bubble—head down, stuck on their phone—but I also think that people keep their eyes and ears open. Perhaps not *all* people *all* of the time, but I am certain that I am not alone when I say that witnessing a disagreement play out in front of me takes precedence over my social media app and what my friend is eating for dinner. This is where the influence we have on strangers comes into play. I think people do pay attention more than we realize. Therefore, why aren't we all continually asking ourselves, "Am I the best version of myself right now?"

Now, you might be thinking, *René, I don't care about what other people think of me. I don't need to please anyone other than myself.* While I do agree that we shouldn't be overly concerned with what others think of us, that is not the point of "being filmed." The idea that we are being filmed for a pretend audience is a great tool because there are people in each of our lives who we want to make proud. YOU get to choose who your pretend audience is! It could be your spouse, children, parents, God, favorite sports team, or even a room full of people like you. Your audience should be anyone who helps you be the best version of yourself. Ultimately, it is *you* who you are making the film for, and it is *you* who needs to be pleased with your actions. At the end of the day, you are the one who has to go to sleep at night and be able to live with yourself.

I don't think many of us realize the degree to which we influence others; or, for that matter, how long our influence may stick with them. For example, one of my first babysitting jobs was when I was in junior high. Lisa, a mother of 3-year-old twins, was hoping to have 2 hours for herself in the afternoons, so I helped after school. From her, I learned about "time-outs." Should one of the twins need a time-out, they had to sit on the stairs for 3 minutes (one minute for every year). This was my first experience with time-outs, and I loved that discipline could be done calmly and without anger. Almost 40 years later, I still remember her and the influence she had on me and my parenting.

The influence each of us portrays can be just as powerful. As I said earlier, we may not realize who is paying attention at any given moment. We may not even realize that our influence could impact someone for their entire lifetime. Here I am, writing about Lisa, the neighbor I babysat for nearly 40 years ago. I am positive that there are also people who you can look back on as being a powerful influence in your life, whether that be positive or negative. That is why, for me, my pretend audience watching my life "film" plays such an important role in being the best person I can be.

Alas, no one is perfect. You may feel that there are times when your film needs to go on the cutting room floor, but that's part of life! We can learn from our mistakes and failures and move on to be better. Only when we strive to learn and grow are we at our best. And only then can we be a positive influence on ourselves and others.

It's exciting, right? Knowing how important you and your influence really are? At least, I hope by now you can appreciate how your influence is the most valuable thing you have to offer.

Now, it's your time to shine! Show the world your powerful and positive influence. Get out there and start making a great film—one that you can be proud of and feel good about. Not only will you feel good on the inside, but you will most likely show someone else what being cognizant of their actions and influence can do. It's really a win-win scenario.

I hope you enjoy learning how to be a positive influence for your teams! I may be biased, but Brian is my favorite author of all time.

Even if he did fire me. *Wink.*

Introduction

Picking up where the first book in the *"I" in Team* series left off, this book is a continuation of your journey to learn more about how to be a positive influence for yourself and your teams. We say "teams" as a plural because we believe you belong to *several* teams. You belong to your team of family members and coworkers, at a bare minimum, and you might also belong to a sports team or club, or an organization or a non-profit. Anytime you join one or several other individuals in pursuit of a common goal, you become a team. In our first book, we took you on an internal journey to discover your foundation, who you are, and how you are perceived. In the book you hold in your hands, we want to help you understand how to apply the knowledge learned in the first book while striving to be a positive influence.

In fact, one of the questions born from writing our first book, *Individual Influence: Find the "I" in Team*, was, "What do I do with the influence I have? How can I 'be' the 'I' in team?" And, as we shared, our words, actions, decisions, thoughts, and reactions, or lack thereof, *do* have an influence. They influence us and those around us, rippling away like the rings around a rock freshly thrown into the water. That influence can impact various singular individuals, but they can also impact teams/groups or what we like to call "Individuals" (which we characterize with a capitalized "I").

Another way we can look at the power of influence is through the lens of the "butterfly effect." Boiled down, the butterfly effect essentially explains that even one small action can cause a ripple effect and lead to a much larger, greater action. With the butterfly effect, one generally does not know if their actions, words, or reactions cause an influence-ripple, nor do they usually know *who* they may affect. By understanding that each of us matters, as does the influence we create, we can live more consciously aware of the effect we have on others, even if we can't see those effects.

Additionally, we have our own perceptions of the world around us. Our perceptions are based upon a multitude of variables, from how we grew up to where we are now. Our cumulative life experience and how we choose to view our life's progression create our perception. To better understand our words, actions, thoughts, perception, and influence, we must first slow down. Slowing down allows us to examine our past, from our earliest memories to our more recent ones, in a comprehensive way. The process of self-reflection is different for everyone, which is why the first book focuses on a multi-method approach to self-reflection that is inclusive. Understanding ourselves, what influences us, and what we influence allows us to be our best selves.

You may be asking yourself how you can take more control of the influence you have. I have personally recognized that my thoughts and actions influence what happens in my life and the lives of those around me. From the moment I wake up to when I come home for dinner, every interaction and thought influences other individuals and myself.

As I pointed out in my first book, there is a word that I am notorious for using, even when it seems I am clearly speaking about myself: We. I have been known for using the word "we" when speaking about my own work because there haven't been many things in my professional career that I alone have provided; I have always had a team supporting me. In this book, you will see the use of "we" when it may seem that I am only talking about myself. Additionally, I often confuse people with my interchangeable use of "I" and "we," but I am unsure of the exact moment I made this shift. It was around the time one of my partnerships was terminated, and I had an overwhelming epiphany about how my actions contributed to that termination.

The conscious shift from "I" to "we" improved my relationships across all aspects of my life, and now I find myself specifically pausing at the use of the word "I," wondering if it's possible that there is a better way to make individual statements without clouding context or the details.

My goal for this book, and this series, is to convey my belief that our individual influence is something we must be mindful of, because influence is our single greatest responsibility in life. Our individual influence begins before we are born, when our parents discover our existence. Despite knowing nothing about us, they do know we will be an individual they are responsible for.

Influence goes both ways; just as we influence our parents when they first discover our existence, our parents influence us. In *Individual Influence,* I discussed the influence of being born to a young mother and father who, while loving me, were still unaware of who or what they really wanted to be or do with their lives. Their ability to live in a reactive environment established much of who I am today. In this book, I will continue sharing lessons on how to be a positive influence through the lens of personal storytelling. I believe storytelling and learning from others' mistakes is one of the most effective ways we learn.

Positive Influence was written to help you build on your foundation so that you can be the best leader for yourself and others. You may even notice that we revisit some topics discussed in the first book. We do this because there are some topics and lessons that are so large that they require further explanation, depending on which perspective you take. In *Individual Influence*, we explored the perspective of finding your foundation; in this book, we are looking from the perspective of being a positive influence. Each topic discussed here is designed to help you accentuate your strengths and overcome challenges that may be holding you back from being a positive, influential leader. We also want to push you to learn and explore new ideas that we did not cover in *Individual Influence*, topics that are directly attributed toward leadership that can be applied to any environment.

The adage is that there is no "I" in team; however, our entire series is centered around the concept that there *is* an "I" in team. The main definition of "I," in terms of our philosophy, is *influence*; however, another smaller, still important, definition of "I" is *individual/Individual*. We defined these terms in the first book as Individual, characterized with a capitalized "I," meaning more than one person or a group, and an uncapitalized individual, referring to a single person.

When you work alone, you are an individual. When you work on a team toward a goal, together, you become an Individual. Therefore, all teams are considered Individuals. We define Individuals as companies, communities, families, friend groups, sports teams, countries, and more. When you work, no matter the field, your work represents more than just yourself. In your workplace, you represent your foundation, your values, and your experiences, as well as your influence. Your influence on others demonstrates that which has influenced you and continues to influence you.

In *Individual Influence*, my goal was to provide a foundation of understanding to support individuals in being their best selves and defining their individual influence. Life is not about who has the most. Very few people will remember you for what you tangibly possessed; most will remember the influence you had on them (and others). That is why you remember how people made you feel or what they said, as opposed to remembering what they wore. This stems from who you are and who you decide to be as a human being.

Now is the time to determine what kind of influence you want to have. *Positive Influence: Be the "I" in Team* will attempt to lead you toward being a positive influence on all your teams. If you wish to do so, you must take the foundational understanding of yourself—which you learned in *Individual Influence*—and begin to apply that understanding to the lessons in the pages that follow. Some lessons we will tackle are keeping your composure, taking the high road, finding balance, being fair and objective, and not taking things for granted. The lessons contained herein are meant to guide you on a path toward a better and more sustainable life. It's time to be a more positive influence for yourself and your teams.

Chapter 1
Influence

"You don't have to be a 'person of influence' to be influential. In fact, the most influential people in my life are probably not even aware of the things they've taught me."
—Scott Adams

We risk diminishing the value of our influence when we ignore the influence we have on others and focus solely on the influence we have on ourselves. This is something that can happen to anyone, and it probably happens to you from time to time. We can recognize this tendency in those who are consistently selfish or think the world revolves around them. Those who purposely ignore their influence can create chaos and destruction in their lives and the lives of others. By understanding our influence and using it properly, we must understand that we are a product of all that influences us.

As you prepare for this reading journey, we have one request to ask of you: be honest with yourself. We aren't going to ask you to change anything about yourself (unless you want to); we just ask that if there are some negative or not-so-positive traits about yourself (as defined by you), that you be honest about them. In order to learn from our writings and beliefs, and to be the best influence you can be, you must be honest. As with our first book, we will share stories and experiences that have happened throughout the course of our lives.

These stories resonate with our belief that "individual" and "influence" are synonymous and hold the keys to being a positive leader for yourself and your teams. This stems from our philosophy that you cannot have influence without the individual and vice versa; they are so closely associated that their mere mention brings the other to mind. We believe it would be impossible to be an individual and not have influence. Being alive means being influential. As previously noted, your influence begins at conception. When you were born, you created a larger Individual, your family, and together you all begin to influence the lives of those around you.

As you age, you begin to join other Individuals—work, sports teams, community service, friend groups, and any other team-like environment where we have an opportunity to work with other individuals. For my team, my Individual Advantages (DBA IA Business Advisors) team, I have not always been a great leader or peer. I do not pretend to be anything but human in my ability to make bad decisions and allow other internal and external influences to affect how I influence myself and others. I strive to do and be my best for all my teams and anyone I influence, but as a human, I make mistakes daily. I learn from my mistakes and expect my teams, peers, and family to hold me accountable. My hope in telling you this is that you will not be hard on yourself when you recall or make mistakes or failures. Mistakes and failures are springboards for opportunity and learning.

Opportunities to influence positively are abundant when we work on a team. Most of these opportunities stem from the differences, shortcomings, and advantages (or strengths) we have. We live in a world where we need to objectively and constructively celebrate and embrace our differences. One of the beautiful things about working on a team is that you almost never have the same shortcomings or advantages as other team members. This means that the team can grow and become stronger as team members support each other and make up for areas that are lacking. Therefore, teams can work together in the ebb and flow of advantages and differences to make a balanced team effort potentially more successful and influential. My team has developed most of the solutions to the challenges I bring with me, and I embrace their efforts to overcome my individual issues as their efforts were developed under a certain amount of duress (negative influence). To offer an example of this, one such trait of mine comes to mind.

Early in my career, I was a bit of a lone ranger. I micromanaged as much as I could, to a fault. My micromanaging tendencies weren't such that I was hovering over my team's shoulder 24/7, but that I believed my solutions for our clients were always right and that my team should follow my solutions blindly. From day one, I made assumptions about my solutions. I assumed my team understood the context of every problem we were hired to solve and would therefore understand, in detail, my solutions. My assumption and unwillingness to budge created obstacles for my team during the implementation process of our projects. Despite the repeated scope issues my team identified, I continued micromanaging the solutions and then left my team to their own devices to figure out the rest.

Essentially, I managed the clients and micromanaged the solutions for our clients. I would then hand off the project and solutions to my team but wouldn't allow them to drift from the solutions I had created. Interestingly enough, our projects always ended successfully, although our path was full of obstacles. As we grew, I began to recognize the issues I was creating in our team culture through my micromanaging tendencies. Unfortunately, my ego and hope to be seen as a leader got in the way of me acting like a *true* leader. I ignored my observations and doubled down on my position to go unchallenged.

It wasn't until 2002 that the culmination of this immense character and leadership flaw came to light. It was after 9/11, and external influences such as the drastically altered economy and changes in how we viewed security as a nation emphasized my views on leadership and shed some light on how much I was allowing my ego to negatively influence myself and my teams. I had a moment of clarity and realized how damaging my micromanaging tendencies and ignorance were to my influence. The challenges our business began to face required more objective thought and input from our team, not the opinion and interpretation of just myself. I was used to leading a team that had almost no disruptions and no challenges; we were best in class, and leading is easy when there is minimal conflict. The new economy bred challenges in delivering our work and meeting objectives, which required more depth. It was amazingly apparent that my leadership tendencies and ignorance were the primary instigators to the challenges we faced. This is when I started to consider what influence really means and how we can use our influence for the benefit of ourselves and our teams. I felt the responsibility to share this philosophy with others as well so that they, too, could begin to feel the weight of their responsibility.

To be a positive influence on your teams, you need to consider more than just yourself. One of the key traits of someone who has a positive influence is the ability to view themselves and situations multi-dimensionally. To be the "I" in team and reach great heights in whatever area of influence you choose, you must be committed and put forth effort for more than just yourself. It is not sustainable to try to always be the sole beneficiary of success. In fact, you are rarely the only one affected by success (this relates to our philosophy on the use of the word "we"). Success is often a team collaboration, and the win should be celebrated as such—as a team. I have a history of negative influence to learn from, and I am sure you can think of moments to learn from in your own life. Therefore, I have more context to use as a guide to be a better leader.

As you read through these chapters, you will begin to see the puzzle pieces of your teams and how they fit together. This will help you see how you can be the "I" in your teams, and how to tailor that as a unique individual. I believe that using my own life experiences as guidance will help you become a more successful and positive influence, especially in situations where inherent human action can interfere and short-circuit positive influence and experiences. There is a place for each of us in this world; we should celebrate our differences to provide positive influence for ourselves and others.

Before we dive in, remember this important truth: You don't always have to be in complete control, and it is in your spirit as a human being to collaborate with others.

Communication

Communication is something that will be addressed throughout the *"I" in Team* series because, although it still seems to be the most common and biggest failure of humans, it is the greatest asset of leaders and influencers. The importance of communicating with others and ourselves is grossly under-appreciated by some, completely misunderstood by others, and taken for granted by many. Communication is the foundation of being the "I" in team, so each lesson in this book heavily relies on communication.

Communication is more than just speaking or providing information. It's about listening and interpreting the ways in which others communicate with us. It's how we analyze information and disseminate that information to others. Context also plays a huge role in communication—let's not forget about body language, tone, and inflection. If we can control how we communicate, we can control our influence as leaders.

I believe that one of the first things people judge about us when they meet us is our ability to communicate. How we speak, write, look, and react all affect how and what we communicate. The impression we provide someone when we first meet them is a form of communication that can have a dramatic influence on how any future relationship with them progresses. How we present ourselves to others is vitally important, and most of us attempt to take great care in managing our first impressions with others, in many different ways.

Communication doesn't solely rely on what you say or write; you communicate who you are by how you look, how your team looks, and how your company looks. To give you an example, in our friend group when we lived in Colorado, there was a "typical" management consultant. He worked for a progressive management firm that did business with very high-profile clients. We never hit it off, and from 1999 to 2005, he was dismissive, standoffish, and arrogant. There came a time after we moved to Oregon that this man came up in a business conversation. I learned that we didn't hit it off because he didn't respect my grassroots approach toward consulting and lacked respect for me because I didn't come up through the ranks of a big consulting firm. I have lost several potential clients because I didn't come across as the "typical" management consultant.

Image carries a lot of influence in terms of communication, but my team and I decline to pretend to be something we are not to be accepted by the industry. Throughout IA's history, we have lost clients because our offices were not what the client expected. IA often integrates our offices with other entities we have influence over (equity or long-term responsibility, like fractional executive services). When we lived in Oregon, we had our office space inside the building of our biggest client at the time. Our team either shared my office or worked in the adjacent employee break area. Meeting potential clients there prohibited IA from doing business with several organizations because they believed we couldn't possibly be effective due to our "image." Even after explaining our choices in depth, and the breadth of our capabilities across multiple states and nations, they still refused. They couldn't understand who IA was—who we were was lost in the image of a group of people sharing an office space on the second floor of a bowling alley.

Another example of IA being dismissed due to superficial communication is how we present ourselves physically. Traditional management consulting firms have steep dress codes, often wearing suits or something akin to suits. The idea behind this is that if you wear a suit, you look like you know what you're doing (key term here is "look like"), as if somehow wearing a suit actually does make you better at what you do. While image does matter in some contexts, as consultants, it's important to realize that not all clients *want* you to wear a suit. I was once told I was too dressed up when I wore a suit to a client meeting; in fact, I was dismissed and told to come back when I had dressed down. To some, image matters when communicating, but it does not denote expertise or ability. It's their ego that prevents clients from working with us because of image.

Our advisory firm is relatively small, with fewer than 50 employees. We are down-to-earth, sometimes to a fault. We have reasonable prices based on the markets we serve and the affordability of that market; our goal is to help small businesses make it, not be a burden or risk. We are familial and tight-knit; we treat our teams and clients like they are family. However, these things don't limit our work ethic or our ability to succeed. What we do is fair, and we don't believe in developing an air of pretentiousness just to humor others' preconceived opinions about us or our abilities. A fancy suit, car, or business card does not make you a good advisor, person, or leader. Unfortunately, you will face these issues as a leader often. Your ability to be a good leader is, however, based on your ability to communicate that you are the best option for the job. Understanding your environment and its idiosyncrasies can make or break a relationship, and you need to decide if those influences are important and worth your effort.

It seems we spend our lives trying to manage these false impressions of ourselves just to get people to like us. How we manage others' impressions of us can be an advantage or a disadvantage, and it's our job as a leader to control that. In this way, we communicate to the world what we are all about.

There are several other methods of communication that we must recognize, and our influence depends on our ability to manage the forms we use as individuals and as a team.

Micro-Communications

As we've explored a bit already, communication is not just about how we talk or write. However, direct communication can be the most potent and influential. Verbal communication used to only be possible face-to-face or on the phone, but now we have video conferencing, which can be conducted from anywhere in the world zwith access to the Internet and a computer, phone, or tablet. Video conferencing adds a layer that only face-to-face communication used to have: body language. Combining our body language with tone and inflection means that we have a powerful communication tool to use our influence.

After the world was rocked by the COVID-19 pandemic, the video-conferencing industry boomed. Teams and individuals all over the world were forced to adapt meetings, classes, seminars, conferences, and so much more to a video-conferencing medium, in addition to relying on email, text, and other impersonal, technological means of communication. With human interaction becoming increasingly virtual, we must remain mindful of how our communication is perceived by others.

Body language is the most difficult to understand, adjust to, and accept. You can't see yourself, so it's hard to understand how others perceive you. It's kind of like hearing your own voice on a recording; for most of us, it's unrecognizable and just weird. The first step to managing your body language is to slow down, remain in the present moment, and be aware. When you are aware, you can attempt to understand how your body language affects others. Thus, you have more control.

Your ability to keep your composure or maintain your emotions when communicating affects your influence greatly. I don't typically hide my emotions well. I am relatively transparent when my emotions are piqued. However, sometimes my emotions can be misread. For example, when I am deep in thought, those around me have noted I have a scowl on my face. At first, I shrugged this off. Over time, I have begun to realize that how I look has an influence on those around me. In fact, my daughter, Mary, has been described as having RBF (resting bitch face).

This "face at rest" scowl can cause others to lose their confidence when approaching either of us. Peers, subordinates, and clients can find it uncomfortable to approach when our faces say so much. However, we aren't always aware that our faces are saying we are "angry," we are just deep in thought. I think many of you can relate to this. Managing how others see us, even when we are lost in thought, is important to how we communicate. It wasn't until I put a camera in front of my face and started filming vlogs that I noticed my own body language and deep-thought scowl.

You may be wondering how to overcome body language issues during a video conference. I believe this is where understanding your image and actively identifying how you look is critical. For me, I always keep open the small image of myself so I can regularly check to ensure my physical state isn't conveying anything I don't want it to. I want the other parties to feel my interest and participation. Similarly, if I hear something during the call that I know will affect my emotional state, I am honest about that as soon as possible to ensure that any facial cues I give are not taken out of context. Being honest about your emotions and thoughts doesn't need to be negative. It will actually have a positive impact as you strive to keep everyone on the same page with you.

Another tip for positive body language is to be aware of how you hold your body in general, more than just the look on your face. Things like relaxing your shoulders and putting them back, not crossing your arms or legs, and maintaining eye contact all contribute to how you are perceived in conversation. One of the best ways to give positive body communication is to look relaxed, attentive, and joyful. If you can be engaged *and* look engaged, you will give others a more relaxed perception of you. When you can make others feel like you are calm and approachable, the remainder of your communication will come more easily.

The words you use and the information you absorb affect your body language. In fact, the words you speak and those that are spoken to you are the biggest catalysts for body language. The context or topics are the fuel. When you combine positive body language with precise words, you become a powerful influence. This means that you must always prepare yourself to communicate. From the moment you wake up, you are communicating who you are, how you are feeling, and what you are thinking about, even if you don't use words.

Encode and Decode Communication

Part of the preparation for communication is knowing who you are going to be communicating with. Who someone else is, and how they interpret communication, will play a huge role in how you engage them. If you don't know the person you are interacting with, there are some risks associated with how they perceive your communication. It's best to communicate with new people in a neutral, socially acceptable way until you get to know them better.

For example, there are people in the world who strongly prefer direct and "harsh" communication in order to continue with their work. These people prefer to be communicated to without all the bells and whistles or the cherry on top; they don't pay attention to, or mind, the negative emotions associated with that style. On the flip side, there are those who are more sensitive to emotion and need to receive communication in a calmer, more indirect manner. There is no right or wrong way to want to be communicated with, but there is a right and wrong way to communicate with someone. You must know who you are communicating with in order to discover the best way to approach them.

If you want to have better communication with someone, ask them what they think of your communication style. Have—hold onto your seats—*open* communication with them. Approach them and ask, "I am trying to learn more about how I communicate. Can you share with me some issues we might have?" You may need to give some examples because if the person you are talking to also struggles with communication, they may not know *why* you are requesting information.

Ask them about your body language, tone, inflection, and ability to give context and information. You may also ask how you act when they communicate with you. Gaining a better understanding of yourself from another's point of view will allow you to have a more positive influence on them and others. It will also help them understand how you communicate. If the other person brings up any issues, clarify the reasons behind your communication. If you wish to change the issues brought up, ask how you might do that.

You must also know the facts or what you are talking about when you communicate. It is critical to perform your due diligence and understand the topic being discussed, even if it's only in a cursory way. You don't always have to have all the information; sometimes, you enter conversations with the intent to learn new information. However, if you are the person delivering the information, be prepared to educate those who wish to learn from you.

Communication changes slightly when the audience is more than one person. This is what mass marketing, politicians, and the media do. They can speak to one issue or cause and reach several different communication styles. When attempting to speak to a mass audience, think about who they are and their purpose for being there. What are their commonalities? Why are they congregated to hear you speak? After answering these questions, speak to them in a way that addresses the group as a whole. Ensure that your presentation discusses the overall theme and present your facts in the proper context. Never assume that everyone gets what you are saying. Try to give everyone all the facts, even if it becomes repetitive to some. Allow for open questions and make sure everyone gets on the same page. Your main objective is to positively influence this group by giving them all the information they came to hear.

If your team is having a meeting, get everyone focused and present for the meeting. This will not only make all of you more efficient, but it will make the communication process smoother. If your team is presenting something to a client, have a pre-meeting to practice how you will communicate with that client. If you find that people are distracted or are distracting others, dismiss them for the moment. Your goal isn't to alienate them from the information completely; circle back and deliver the information to them at a time when they are more readily available to receive it.

There are times when we fail to see things right in front of our faces because we aren't remaining present or using situational awareness. This includes when we are communicating with people who don't seem to be understanding what we are saying. This kind of awareness requires some amount of emotional intelligence and the ability to read people. We understand the context from which our words are coming from, but it may become lost on those who do not have the same context.

Having clarity about our thoughts and the conversation means that we need to be ready to identify when we have "lost someone." Go back and find which bits of information they are missing and fill them in. If they don't know where they are lost, ask them questions to determine their level of understanding on the topic and start from there. We want to ensure that they understand the topic with the facts we have so that they don't attempt to fill in the gaps with their own assumptions. This can create potential issues that will result in poor communication down the road.

A huge part of communication is listening, which we will discuss in greater detail in a later chapter. As a business consultant, I try to listen twice as much or more than I talk. When we listen, we learn—and we can learn *a lot* about a person when we observe them. I find it fascinating to see the similarities and differences in communication around the world. Some societies embrace animated communication. In certain parts of Asia, Africa, and the Middle East, I have observed very animated discussions between people, sometimes even appearing borderline aggressive. I myself have found it difficult to match that animation when engaged with cultures that value it. I've even been accused of not being interested or engaged in a relationship because of my inability to become overly animated when engaged with cultures that value that kind of communication. Cultural differences in communication become an issue for both parties if neither side considers the cultures and context of the other.

When this happens to me—and it has recently—I take the opportunity to communicate more openly about the fact that I tend to show little emotion in discussions with people I don't already have an established relationship with. I am very much interested in that conversation, and I am also interested in learning how to better communicate with that person. I am open to learning more about how people from that culture communicate, and I don't wish for my observing, quiet nature to get in the way of a relationship blooming. This almost always disarms the negative aspects of our slight miscommunication, gets us back to the topic at hand, and strengthens the relationship.

Having open communication and maintaining our composure when we are presented with negative facts about ourselves is key to having a positive influence. The only way we can get through anything together as a team, and work toward the same goal, is to ensure that everyone is on the same page. It's always better to be on the same page as a team. We can't achieve our goals, hit milestones, or be our best selves if we are all moving in different directions. This starts and ends with communication. When we can maintain our composure through difficult situations of uncomfortable communication, we begin to be the "I" in team.

Key Takeaways: Communication

- Communication is more than just speaking: it includes listening to others' words; interpreting their body language, tone, and inflection; and understanding how they interpret you. It's about understanding your environment and knowing how to communicate in that environment to receive the outcome you desire.
- First impressions are a unique type of communication that signal to the other person what they may expect from you in the future. This is why first impressions are typically seen as important events.
- Be extra mindful of communications you conduct via technology, including texts and emails, so that tone, inflection, and body language are not lost. Do not give your reader an opportunity to fill in those spaces with emotions that you may not have intended.
- When speaking to a mass audience, keep in mind that your audience members are diverse and will have different values and communication styles. This means that you will need to tailor your message to reach everyone on some level so they feel connected.
- If you find that others are becoming a distraction to the message being delivered, ask them to leave and deliver the information to them at a time when they are ready to receive it.

- If you recognize that you've lost someone while communicating with them, start asking them questions to better understand their current knowledge base so you can help them get on the same page as you. Doing this will avoid them using assumptions to fill in the gaps.

Composure/Self-Control

There are several ways to define composure or self-control, and most of those differences in definition stem from one's perception of what composure or self-control is. To some, maintaining composure means having a lack of animation or excitement; to others, it is possible to remain composed while also being animated or excited. This section's message will vary depending on your perception of what maintaining composure means, but for the purpose of this lesson, we will start with a general understanding of what it means to maintain composure or self-control.

The root of maintaining composure or self-control is understanding your personal, negative impulses and having them under control or hidden during times of influence. For example, when dealing with an individual who is displaying anger toward you, it can be difficult to remain calm as our fight or flight response kicks in. We may be tempted to hit back, say something mean, or simply leave the room. Yet maintaining composure in negative, public situations can end up saving you issues to deal with later—even if those issues are just internal feelings of guilt. Those who remain composed even under a certain amount of duress not only demonstrate quality behavior in front of peers but can also be more productive and give better perspective to everyone under their influence.

One dramatic example of maintaining composure with a positive outcome happened in 2004. We were hired to work with a company in the San Francisco area that had been in the same family for 6 generations. We were tasked with helping them transition to the next generation of ownership as well as making their manufacturing and distribution process more efficient. Most of the management team had been with the company for 10 years or more, and some for 20 or more. This meant that we had several employees who were firmly rooted in the status quo. We knew it would be difficult to influence them through the changes being recommended and implemented.

Two of the areas we started with were human resources and distribution/shipping. I was leading the distribution-enhancement project, and the man I was assigned to work with (head of shipping) had been with the company for over 15 years. Our relationship started off on a positive note. However, by the second week of our project, my team and I were working in segregated offices in our client's facility. First thing one morning, the head of shipping walked into our office and proceeded to cuss me out, using expletives including "mother fucker."

After his outburst, he just turned and walked away. He didn't even yell; his tone was neutral and flat. My teammates looked at me. Those working on the HR program, having observed the altercation, noted that it seemed they were going to need to put some of their work into play sooner than anticipated. We always have issues with employees at the beginning of projects if our work directly impacts their day-to-day functionality. Change is uncomfortable for most people. Change disrupts routine, and most of us are usually fairly comfortable within our routines. Employees usually deal with this discomfort in covert ways to keep things as they are or to subvert our authority by rallying peers to prove our recommendations will fail.

Having just come off a great weekend with my family and being in a good mood, I decided that we would just ignore the issue that day and keep working. Later that morning, when I had to meet with the shipping department and the shipping manager, there was not a single mention of the incident, nor were there any issues generally associated with projects like this. I thought the issue had resolved itself and looked forward to working with him and his team.

The next day, the IA team arrived early for a team meeting, and it was noted that the previous day's work had proceeded business as usual after the strange verbal assault. About 15 minutes after our meeting ended, the same manager walked into our office and cussed me out again in a very controlled tone, just as he had the day before. One of my teammates seemed distressed because she feared it could turn into something more aggressive. Another thought we should speak to management. I decided to do nothing. I wasn't sure what was causing the issue, but while we were working together the day before, everything was fine.

Well, the same exact thing happened the next day. He just walked in, cussed me out, and left. I finally decided it was time to go visit him about the issue. I was beginning to feel anxious and almost angry myself. My only rule at IA is that if you are going to cuss at me, warn me first. We all need to be open to accepting the negative rants of people we may negatively influence; there is just a correct way to do it. I walked into his office and, as he had the previous two days, he greeted me normally and looked ready to work. I sat down and asked him why he came into my office and cussed at me for three days straight.

His response was that he had been coming to work every day for 15 years, and in that time, he had almost zero change to his job. He knew what to expect, good and bad, from the people he worked with and the customers and vendors that supported him. He enjoyed his morning drive to work in peace with the anticipation of knowing exactly what to expect from his day. Since IA started working on the change programs—which he fully understood would be beneficial to him and the company in the future—every morning, he was full of dread and uncertainty. He felt angry after stewing during his drive, and he figured that it would be more productive to get his feelings out. Basically, his cussing me out in the morning helped him move on with his day and be more productive.

I was a little shocked at his honesty, and as I sat there, I could tell he was looking at me without any malice. He was working the best he could to ensure that we, as a team, could and would be successful. By both of us finding a way to maintain our composure, we found a way to ensure team success. Eventually, he stopped coming in to cuss me out, and the IA team learned a good lesson. There was a lot to be said about composure and how to read through words spoken with calm presentation. Our client's team also learned that communication allowed us to move forward, even if that communication seemed negative. I personally learned that composure is so much more than just a moment; it is part of who a person is and defines them in many ways.

By losing composure or self-control, under most situations, it means having an influx of emotion. Regardless of whether those emotions are positive or negative, they do tend to compromise composure. Individuals who can stay composed, and are thus operating at a more level baseline of emotion, can usually get more done. By staying composed, one can stay focused. That level of focus is what allows individuals to be more productive than their counterparts who may be distracted by a lack of composure.

It could also mean conducting yourself in a manner that, while you may be internally screaming, you display calmness on the outside. Having control of your language and tone, while still not feeling internally calm, shows a certain amount of self-control. It is fair to assume that people need to be offered ways to manage their composure. Since life can be stressful, which wears down composure and self-control, we all need an outlet for negative feelings so that we maintain composure.

Two of the best ways I have found to keep composure and have self-control in an emotional situation are (1) to remind myself of my influence and the effect my words and actions have on others, and (2) to think of a "happy place" or a moment in my life when I was calm. For me, my "happy place" is when I am with René and/or the kids, or doing one of my hobbies, like cooking, riding my PWC (Sea-Doo jet-ski), or writing about my passion (influence and the (I)individual).

To be honest with you, keeping composure and self-control in the moment is personal and different for everyone. Try to remind yourself that there will be an appropriate time for you to decompress and review the issue through a less emotional lens. Relaxing is the personal part. Some individuals love meditation and yoga, while others relax by starting an art project or reading a book or listening to music or other audible media. Perhaps you love scrolling social media or talking to a friend on the phone. I urge you to find what makes you feel calm and centered as soon as possible so that, in the future when you are faced with maintaining your composure and self-control, you will have a potential outlet to diffuse emotional situations.

Composure does not only apply to negative emotions. I have seen people lose their composure over positive things, and that loss of composure can be just as distracting as a negative reaction. Some of the positive things that can distract us from our composure include over-celebrating or taking things for granted. I've known people who have celebrated positive news or events so much that they overindulge and end up dealing with issues like a DUI or setting too high of an expectation due to bragging.

Another common example of losing composure in a way that is detrimental, yet seemingly positive, is in sports. I once watched a guy who thought he scored a touchdown but never crossed the goal line; he dropped the football only to have a defender pick it up and run the other way for a touchdown. There are other examples like this where athletes stop playing to celebrate what they think are great plays only to learn that the play failed, and the loss of composure cost them points or even the game.

Composure is about maintaining control over your emotions in a way where you don't lose focus, control, or situational awareness. This doesn't mean that you can't celebrate, become angry, and express your emotions vibrantly. As a leader and when working with a team, it is important to maintain your ability to know what is going on around you both physically and emotionally. How you compose yourself will have an influence on others.

As I noted above, one of the policies we have at IA is that we understand moments when our team members need to allow for a loss of composure and vent. Our policy is that if they give a warning before launching into a break of their composure, then they are free to do so. The policy was originally put in place to ensure there was not a complete breakdown in composure. I personally hate surprises, and when confronted by those that include a loss of composure, there are rarely good results. This next story doesn't put me in the best light, but it's a great example of why we need to keep our composure.

In 1998, we began working with a partner company that sold computer hardware, so I found myself at their offices a lot. While our two companies were partnered, I didn't get along well with their sales team. So much so that a couple of them decided to recommend another IT company to perform the work. One day, while I was there to discuss the projects we were working on, the salesman I had sold our work to informed me that they would be offering the work to our competitor.

I was amazingly angry, as we had already agreed to a partnership. As I got angrier, he got angrier, and the argument progressed from professional to personal. His derogatory comments went from being aimed at me to being aimed at my team and our families (which is when I lost my composure). As I walked out, I hit the wall next to his office and ended up putting my fist through the thin drywall. The moment I did this, I immediately came out of my rage and snapped back into professional mode. I was embarrassed. I walked into the company's president's office, told him what happened, and called to have the repairs made.

As I made my way back to my office, I reflected on what happened, and on a few other instances where a loss of composure had caused embarrassment. I realized that stress and insecurity drove these emotions. It was after the wall incident that I decided to create a way for people to have a safe way to vent. In these times, my team can be as loud, obnoxious, improper, or insubordinate as they want to be. We have a space of no judgment where I honestly commend them for maintaining their composure where it is needed. It is impractical to assume that everyone must always maintain their composure; by giving my team a safe space to vent their frustrations, they are able to continue their work with self-control.

I find that by giving my team an out for their negative emotions, they can keep their composure for longer. When they know they have a safe space to vent, they can keep their negative emotions inside and wait. Otherwise, they may be more likely to lose their composure if they don't anticipate being able to vent. If you do not have a safe space to vent and are in a position where you may lose your composure, ask yourself if you would be happy taking the low road or the high road. The low road will bring nothing but negativity, but the high road puts you above it all and allows you to remain a positive influence. Vent to a friend, family member, or team member, just give them a warning first. Remember where you are using your influence and who you are influencing.

Key Takeaways: Composure/Self-Control

- Composure is about maintaining enough self-control to not lose focus, emotional stability, control, or awareness. This doesn't mean that you can't celebrate or express your emotions.
- When you are in a stressful situation, displaying the ability to remain calm and composed can help influence others to also stay calm (while demonstrating your ability to stay productive).
- Two of the best ways to keep composure and have self-control in an emotional situation are (1) to remind yourself of your influence and the effect your words and actions have

on others, and (2) to think of a "happy place" or a moment in your life when you were calm.

- If you do not have a safe space to vent and are in a position where you may lose your composure, ask yourself if you would be happy taking the low road or the high road. The low road will bring nothing but negativity, but the high road puts you above it all and allows you to remain a positive influence.

The High Road

Influential leaders can sometimes feel like they are above everyone, and I don't mean that they think they are better than everyone else. The "high road" is a place that leaders need to travel to differentiate themselves and their organization from other leaders or organizations. Leaders consistently take the high road. It can be lonely and unpopular, but I have yet to find a high road that was not the right road.

The high road, in a nutshell, is when we choose to do what is right, even if it is not the most popular, fun, or exciting thing to do. We may find ourselves standing alone in a room full of people that agree on something popular that does not meet the values of either ourselves or our organizations. Sometimes it means going against the crowd or refusing to make decisions because "it's the way we have always done it." Taking the high road can be stressful, and it can label us as a rebel or even a traitor. Taking the high road does not mean giving up control or allowing other parties to make our decisions for us. When people don't choose the high road, they may seek to justify their actions in a way that compromises their values or minimizes their accountability. As this next story illustrates, taking the high road and maintaining our values is often more beneficial than justifying our actions and walking away.

In the late 1990s, we had an IT company that was growing quickly but struggled to meet financial obligations. I was trying to develop who I was as a leader and found myself faced with a high road situation—twice. One of the perks we had for our team was a 401(k). We matched our team's investments, which required us to make monthly deposits into the employee's account. At the time, I wasn't an administrator, but my partner was, so I delegated all administrative duties to him. My trust in his abilities was without question.

One day, our best technician came to me and accused our company of not making the 401(k) deposits as we had agreed. I was a little taken aback but did not argue with this person. While my trust in my partner made me feel like this person was wrong, my trust in my team made me listen carefully. I assured our technician that I would get to the bottom of the issue and speak to him again. One month later, I had not delivered the answer as promised. (The excuse is irrelevant to the point of the story.) The technician filed a complaint with the Colorado Employment Department for not paying him as agreed, and I was *shocked.* I found out when I was served with a lawsuit; as you may remember, I hate surprises.

I was boiling over with anger. The surprise of being served a lawsuit from an employee for something I understood to be handled by others baffled me. However, I did not react emotionally, primarily because I liked the technician. I slowed down and got into the moment. I thought about it from his perspective and developed some empathy for him; from his perspective, his employer was stealing money from him.

I immediately asked our accounting team to review the issue. We engaged with our 401(k) company and found out how the issue occurred and the cost of the error. However, by this time, the employee had quit. Now, this particular employee was one of the best IT consultants west of the Mississippi. His passion for IT and for helping others is a testament to much of what I write and teach. He understands his purpose and goals, and lives in the moment every day. His exit was a significant loss for our company.

We fixed the issue, which thankfully amounted to less than $100. I contacted our ex-employee and asked to meet with him. I apologized, both personally and professionally, on behalf of our company. He was less concerned about the money and more concerned with our actions related to resolving it. I appreciated that he held us accountable for our technical, emotional, and communication mistakes.

A few weeks later, he contacted me and asked if he could return to the company. I was thrilled he chose us to share his career purpose, so I quickly encouraged him to return. Some felt that we were weak, and it was tough for them to accept his return. I felt that we were strong. Some felt that we were abandoning our obligation to set an example for current and future employees, but I felt like we *were* setting the perfect example. We took the high road. We accepted accountability for our actions, and we rectified them in a way that was equitable for everyone.

As I mentioned earlier, the high road means doing right by people or situations even when it's the least popular thing to do. You don't have to capitulate to others and take the easy way; the high road will be difficult but rewarding. It sometimes means taking the hardest road possible. You may find yourself standing with people who are unpopular. You may find yourself standing alone. You may even find yourself standing up for something that most people don't stand for. In the end, what's right is right. Leaders know this and do everything in their power to do the right thing.

A common question I receive is, "How do I know what the high road is?"

Each of our high roads are built and judged by us, but on the flip side, that means that each of us has a different version of what the high road looks like. What I believe needs to be universal is an affinity toward kindness, honesty, and accountability. If we can be and do our best for those we influence directly and indirectly without violating laws, our values, and the rights of others, then we are on the high road. Of course, there will always be those who disagree with us or will be negatively influenced by our taking the high road. However, when there are more who are positively influenced by our actions or lack of actions, then that is the best path to take.

The high road is the one you need to take to stick to your values, remain a positive influence, and negatively influence those around you as little as possible. Taking the high road means doing what is morally right; it's the road you take to provide the most benefits to the most people. When you take the high road, you fall asleep at night knowing you did all you could, or at least your best. You can go home without regrets for your behavior.

Another question that I am asked is, "How do I take the high road when that road may be counterproductive to the goals and ambitions of the team?" I have faced high road challenges in my area of influence throughout my career, from choosing the side of a partner over that of a client or other unrelated party, to backing my team when a client requests us to do something that is against what we stand for as (I)individuals.

One way we take the high road relates to time management and billing; we do not bill our clients for time we do not spend on them. We have a philosophy in our organization: A minute worked is a minute billed. We believe that our clients deserve to be billed for the work we do, and we measure that work by time. We choose a rate that is based on the expertise of the individual and depth of complexity of the task, but we only bill for actual time spent. We also account for our time with detailed descriptions to offer the best understanding of what we are doing in that time.

We have had some clients feel that billing this way is "nitpicking" them and unfair. They look at a bill and see time billing for 6 or 22 minutes, and they say it's ridiculous. When I explain our philosophy, some clients understand; however, others have requested that we simply bill them in 15- and 30-minute increments, despite the obvious loss to them. The solution for clients who want to be billed in increments such as these is to wait until our time adds up to those increments, but we won't pretend we spent more time on a project for money's sake. This high road costs us money, but it saves our clients' money. We aren't in business to nickel and dime our clients, which is why we choose to take the high road and bill this way.

The high road serves to minimize risk, damage, and loss. That's not to say that there is no risk in taking the high road or that it will never cause damage, because there are always exceptions. The high road can be lonely, as I have learned over the past 19 years. The example above about billing costs me and my team money. I had team members who wanted us to bill up to a rounded increment because it meant a raise or bonus for them; that would mean that I would be paying them for work they did not do, which doesn't fit with my vision for the high road. In the end, you have to determine what is best for you and your influence. The high road will have many rewards, but it can also come at a cost.

Sometimes those in the thick of a decision or actions don't even realize that a decision has gotten them off the high road. One of our previous consultants had amazing promise. He was aggressive but smart. He had the drive to be successful, for himself and our organization. I highly admired this person. Despite some early mistakes and learning mishaps, he was an up-and-coming advisor who seemed to keep raising the bar and churning out better and more thoughtful work. Then, we found out why. He was paying other people to do his work and entering it as his own. He was lying to our clients and to us, and he was benefitting from others' outstanding work, often paying them (in cash) a third to half of what he was being paid. He was putting himself, our company, and our clients at risk.

When I found out, I terminated his work with us as an employee. He decried his entrepreneurial spirit and used ignorance as a justification for his unacceptable actions. However, I was still happy with his individual skills, so I came up with a solution: We helped him properly set up his own company. We then offered him a sub-contractor agreement that protected both parties.

Unfortunately, some people feel that outsmarting others or getting away with unethical behavior is somehow a testament to their acumen in whatever areas they have influence, which is something I did not realize at the time. The relationship with this person ended in an unamicable way: He continued to violate his agreements and do things that only benefited himself. The actions he took were caused by character flaws; however, his inability to be affected by the damages he caused around him will likely continue to prevent him from ever finding the high road.

Generally, the rewards for taking the high road far outweigh the cost, and over time, doing the best thing well is the right thing. The bigger question may be, "How do I *stay* on the high road?" Well, if there is one thing I am sure of, it's that people who decide to get off the high road and take shortcuts will eventually be faced with accountability. The fear of negative accountability and the resulting consequences of not doing the right thing is typically what keeps people on the high road. In my case, I am motivated to stay on the high road because of my principles.

Key Takeaways: The High Road

- Take the high road to stick to your values, remain a positive influence, and negatively influence those around you as little as possible.
- Taking the high road means making a decision that you feel is right, even if it is not the most popular decision. It may mean going against the crowd and standing alone for what you believe in.
- Staying true to your values may mean offending others, challenging the status quo, or becoming unpopular. As long as you can fall asleep at night knowing you did your best, you are on the right path.

Accountability

Accountability is what keeps humanity's tendency to do stupid things in check. When used correctly, it is a powerful tool. Without accountability, people would abuse their influence, and chaos would ensue. In other words, accountability smooths out chaos. It also helps others recognize their blind spots, missteps, and failures and helps them identify how to rectify these things through action or intention. Life has its own way of dealing with accountability, too; many of us call it karma.

Let's first discuss the topic of self-accountability. Holding ourselves accountable for our thoughts, words, and actions is difficult and, to a certain extent, almost impossible. The entire process of accountability challenges our instinct to protect ourselves from harm. In fact, accountability can feel like we are being harmed because it usually hurts in some way.

Thus, self-accountability can prove to be amazingly difficult as it requires an additional level of self-discipline and willpower. The act of holding oneself accountable for something that is wrong but feels good physically, emotionally, or psychologically may be one of the biggest challenges we face. One example of this is drug use.

Using illegal drugs can open a multitude of challenges for any individual; heck, using legal drugs can do the same. There are physical and mental challenges that present themselves when abusing any type of drug. The accountability we have to our own body's physical wellbeing is amplified when battling a drug addiction. Self-accountability doesn't always mean you have to come up with solutions on your own; it could mean simply starting the conversation to outsource the task to someone who will help you protect yourself, such as a doctor.

As I wrote in our first book, I am not naïve when it comes to drugs. The drug world is one of the reasons I am where I am today. To recap a bit of my past from the first book, in high school, I sold drugs at parties, got caught, went to trial, and was given the choice between jail or the Army. I chose the latter, and the structure and discipline I learned from joining the Army paved the way for the rest of my life. I have known several people who have battled drug addiction. The psychological aspects of addiction can prove to be challenging, if not more challenging than the physical. The power certain drugs have on our mental ability to be self-accountable is unparalleled. Drugs can make you do things you never thought you would do, like lie or steal.

Another example of holding someone accountable for lying comes from a past contractor who worked for us. She seemed to always need advances on her paychecks, and back then, I never really paid much attention to her reasons; except that, in her case, her reasons were repetitive (*the-dog-ate-my-homework* kind of stuff). When I started to question her reasoning, she stopped asking for advances. Two months later, we noticed odd purchases from Amazon on our company credit cards; this contractor was buying non-work related items on Amazon, like $600 roller skates. Turns out, she went from making up stories to receive advanced paychecks to charging high-dollar items to our company credit card and then selling them on eBay or Facebook marketplace. We learned she had developed a drug and gambling addiction. I have seen it many times; when self-accountability has been impaired (like in the case of addiction), outsourced accountability is the only way.

For example, Alcoholics Anonymous is a high-profile outsourced accountability group. This organization is built on providing accountability for people who choose to attend in support of a decision that is self-accountable, but the challenges can override an individual's ability to overcome those inner demons. By outsourcing accountability, you gain outside support and encouragement to stay on your chosen path. Today, one only needs to look online or in the App Store to find a plethora of outsourced accountability apps designed to provide third-party support. One that comes to mind is ProHabits, an outsourced accountability platform that helps individuals build healthy habits. Or, if you want to conquer life challenges like weight loss, there are apps like Noom. These programs take the concept of outsourced accountability and commingle it with self-accountability to help affect the change we wish to see.

A true leader who wants to have a positive influence on themselves and others will embrace both self-accountability and outsourced accountability when needed, utilizing both to move them forward and grow. The people I have met who have overcome drug addictions with outsourced accountability generally have a more positive and mindful influence. I believe that some of these people exhibit true leadership qualities that are mirrored by some of the world's most successful leaders.

Religion, spirituality, and morals are other aspects of our lives that can challenge us with accountability. You should not use your religion to justify negative actions as a substitute for self-accountability. Going to church, confession, and prayer shouldn't allow one to "get away with" actions that are otherwise immoral. When my daughter and co-author Mary asked me why I would want to bring religion into a discussion about accountability, I responded that I want to challenge those who use faith as a crutch to behave negatively in life.

However, on the flip side, there are those who use their religion or spirituality as a tool to help them stay accountable. They follow what they believe in, do their best, and know when they have done wrong. The difference here is taking responsibility for their actions and trying to rectify them, versus relying on religion to feel "forgiven" without having any true remorse or attempting to learn from mistakes.

Forgiveness is part of accountability, but it requires participation. Without participation from whomever you wronged, there can be no true forgiveness. True forgiveness, and therefore growth, comes from whomever you hurt. Your wrongdoings cannot be whisked under the carpet to be forgotten because that lacks true accountability. When you do something wrong—something that warrants forgiveness—it often influences someone else and not just yourself. The only way to truly be held accountable is to be honest with the people your wrongdoing may have affected and accept the consequences.

There are lessons embedded in accountability. You can look back at instances when you were held accountable and choose to sulk in negativity, or you can choose to reflect on the lesson and its outcome. One way you can reflect on these lessons is to keep a log of times you have been held accountable. Only by documenting and reviewing your past will you be able to find unique patterns. The lesson will usually be multi-faceted, and if you view the full context of accountability, you may find that it led to something positive. There is a certain amount of maturity and objectivity required to do this. Reflecting on issues that challenged you in the past can instill negative emotions, which is part of the self-accountability process. Embrace the feeling, but don't let it overwhelm you.

To be the "I" in team, you need to understand accountability and your experience of it. You need to be able to apply those lessons in the present and future, as well as to members of your team. It is your responsibility to hold yourself and others accountable. For example, when you allow someone to make errors without any form of accountability, you suggest to them that those actions are acceptable, and they will continue to make the same errors. Repeatedly ignoring a person for doing something wrong only creates negativity. You owe it to that person to help put them on the right path. You can be their outsourced accountability. Otherwise, there are risks and potential for more aggressive accountability (like being suspended or fired) in the future.

Being a leader who doesn't hold others accountable creates potential leaders and team members who will mirror negative actions and not hold themselves or others accountable. This repetitive cycle diminishes the effectiveness of leadership. The trick is to determine what issues need accountability and who holds that responsibility. As a leader, it is your responsibility to hold *yourself* accountable and to determine who holds your *team* accountable.

I would like to share a personal example of accountability and the responsibility you have when in a position of influence. As I wrote in book one, Michele, my stepmother, joined my life when I was in the eighth grade. Our relationship was rocky from the very beginning, but Michele ultimately provided me with the structure and accountability I needed as a troubled child.

Like many adolescents, I was habitually late. Michele, like any other 20-year-old, was struggling with her newfound influence as stepmother to a 13-year-old and mother to a newborn. I challenged her authority in a frustrating way, and generally speaking, I think Michele responded well early on. However, being late was a common issue for me. The rule Michele put in place was simple: If I was late, I would be grounded for one day for every minute I was late. Well, I didn't want to be grounded as a new teenager, so I stopped being late.

I went weeks, maybe even months, without being late on a regular basis. When I was late by just a few minutes, Michele would let it go; once or twice I was grounded for a day, maybe two. While this was excessive in my eyes at the time—of course it was, I was a teenage boy—it was actually quite fair. Then one day, I was with my girlfriend, and we were with her mother at work. It was the weekend, and I had a new baby brother, Justin. Michele had to work, my father was at work, and Michele's father, who was living with us at the time, was unavailable, so it was up to me to babysit Justin with some help from one of our neighbors.

My girlfriend's mother caused us to be late by 15 minutes, through no fault of my own; I was really just along for the ride. My late arrival caused Michele to be late to work, so her retribution was grounding me for 15 days. Herein lies the lesson. Some of you will feel that Michele was right for grounding me, and others will feel that she was not. Was it equitable for me to be grounded for 15 days, since I had zero control over what time I arrived back home? Was this holding me accountable? What lesson did I learn by being grounded over something I had no control over? What consequences resulted from this single action?

Michele told me that I understood the consequences when I agreed to go with my girlfriend in the first place. At 20 years old, I doubt she intended to damage my trust in others, but through her actions, she did. So did my girlfriend's mother, who knew the rules I lived under. I remember arguing that I should not be held accountable for being late if I had no way to be on time.

Michele told me I should not have gone in the first place, unless I was willing to accept the consequences of being late. So, at this point in my life, I changed how I made such decisions. There were a number of occasions when I ran home from school, miles away, to avoid being late, even though my tardiness would have been due to school functions. I understood the consequences of being late, learned what being accountable meant, and altered my behavior in such a way as to live within the context of the rules.

This is just one example of how accountability can affect our behavior. Whether right or wrong, the rules were laid out, and I learned how to adjust my life accordingly. We can all learn from such stories, regardless of our feelings on whether the rules were right or wrong. And, as leaders, we need to ensure that we balance the consequences and delivery of those consequences with the level of accountability we are looking for with each standard or rule in mind.

The consequences of breaking standards or rules should be fair based on the issues at hand. Being grounded for one day for each minute I was late may have had the shock value needed to ensure that I did not frivolously violate that rule. I obviously had violated that rule enough to have my stepmother put the rule in place. However, as a leader, I would need to review the equitable value of such a consequence on anyone who may be late for issues out of their direct control. Equitability—maintaining fairness and impartiality—is important in maintaining morale. For leaders, it is imperative that we understand the value of the lessons to be learned through accountability.

In the end, accountability is a deterrent *and* a tool to influence ourselves and our team to stay focused on the standards and objectives we put in place. It can enhance our focus and enable us to press forward with the support we need. If we can balance the consequences with the rewards, we will reap the benefits. Without accountability, we may find ourselves making other mistakes that only humility can help us avoid.

Key Takeaways: Accountability

- Accountability is challenging yourself or others to remain true to your words and actions by pointing out inconsistencies in hopes of rectifying them in some way. There must also be consequences for these inconsistencies.
- Positive leaders will embrace both self-accountability and outsourced accountability when necessary.
- By documenting and reviewing the previous times you have been held accountable, you may be able to find patterns that are meaningful to you.
- As a leader, holding others accountable is a form of accountability to yourself, the team, and your company. However, in doing so, you must determine the consequence's equitability; determining equitability while holding someone accountable is paramount.

Humility

Humility is the ability to recognize one's self-worth without exaggeration or a need to be boastful. Thus, humble people show their worth through honest action rather than force. Humility allows you to slow down, so you can become in tune with your internal thoughts and feelings. It also allows you to understand and view situations without the weight of negativity. Humility does not mean that you have to be meek or lack a realization of your importance; that would go against what we believe as a core tenet of this series. Instead, being humble strengthens us against those who are arrogant, egotistical, and self-absorbed—those who cannot get out of their own way.

Why do some of us find it difficult to be humble? There is one human characteristic that gets in the way: ego. We discussed ego thoroughly in our first book, as it is something we must try to balance daily. When we don't keep our egos in check, they can run rampant and cause us to speed up, lose connection to our inner thoughts and feelings, and latch onto negativity. Being humble helps us stay grounded while keeping our ego in the shadows.

Being a leader means showing humility where humility is due. In several instances in my life, I have not been humble: my ego, which was really my ignorance, got in the way. Between 1999 and 2002, I was involved in a company that had a tremendous amount of potential. We faced growth challenges, and I decided to take an egotistical approach toward those internal struggles. My first mistake was thinking I could solve the issues on my own.

Part of being a positive leader is knowing that you don't—and shouldn't—have to do anything alone. There are always exceptions to the rule, but one of the great things about being on a team is having other minds to bounce off ideas. The collaboration between team members, that starts with a seedling of an idea, can turn an okay solution into one that is exceptional. Unfortunately, I had not learned this lesson at that time.

In my ego-driven mind, we needed to grow and expand more—more than we already were—to find our way out of the challenges. Unfortunately, I spread myself too thin. I was involved in a plethora of other projects, including working with two of our largest partners to develop new training programs overseas and developing IA as a think tank. I wanted to begin building IA as a foundation to focus on people integration, business process, and technology—all of which were influenced by my doctoral studies. As all these projects were coming together, I assumed the role of CFO, as I had the most accounting experience and understood the issues we faced.

We had a great support team, and my partners trusted me when I told them the situation was under control. But, as you can surmise by how this story is progressing, I did *not* have everything under control. I made decisions alone that should not have been made alone, all because I thought I was the smart one. I degraded my partners, telling myself that they were too technical and lacked the vision to understand what was needed to make this all work; I challenged their business acumen.

As the cracks became canyons and the challenges mounted, I did not wake up or step up. Instead, I circled the wagon and doubled down on my ego. I made decisions that eventually led to the fracturing of our company into three pieces and destroyed our friendships for a lifetime. My ego blinded me from reality. It was a defining moment in my career; from a leadership perspective, it gave me one lesson I desperately needed—a lesson in humility.

The lesson came in the form of guilt, remorse, and empathy. Dividing our companies and hearing the statements made by my partners and team, from their perspective, painted a graphic portrait of the events that transpired. They shared their frustration, hurt, and anger openly, and I felt shame and pain in knowing that I had inadvertently inflicted this on them through my arrogance. They felt that I had nefariously misled them. Furthermore, the pain I caused blinded them to the fact that I was just an arrogant fool who had not yet embraced humility.

From a financial perspective, being humble may not have saved our partnerships. I believe that, regardless of my actions, we may have still decided to break up the company. However, humility would have preserved relationships and friendships that meant something far more than money, something that is too often forgotten. The influence ripple effects of my arrogance created in that moment have continued to exist. To this day, my reputation with the people involved in the breakup is damaged. Unfortunately, we all make decisions that damage our influence, and we have to live with those consequences. It's how we move forward with humility that allows us to grow as positive influential leaders.

Sometimes, the hardest thing to do is to admit that we are wrong. Humbling ourselves can prove to be a difficult feat because our egos prevent us from showing humility, which manifest through anxiety, fear, anger, and more. And it's exponentially more difficult to humble ourselves in front of subordinates. However, this is one of the ways you become a great and positive leader for your team. Respect and trust are built on the foundation of humility.

Humbling yourself in front of your team when you are wrong shows them that not only are you rectifying the issue, but that you are someone they can admire, trust, and rely on when other difficult situations arise. You will set the standard for your team, showing them that you have built a culture where it is okay to admit that they are wrong. When we humble ourselves and encourage our team to remain humble, issues will also be corrected much quicker than keeping everyone in the dark.

Alternatively, humility isn't always about admitting that you were wrong. At times, you have more knowledge and experience on a topic that your team has little or no knowledge or experience in. It can be challenging not to come off as arrogant or a know-it-all when you're the only one with the correct information. If you are ever in a situation where you feel you are the smartest person in the room, one of the best ways to overcome that feeling is to be humble and take a mentorship approach.

Becoming a mentor means you can engage people in new information while being considerate of their current base of knowledge. Instead of aggressively showing off your knowledge, you can create opportunities to engage with your team in a thoughtful way. Teaching and mentoring can tame arrogant tendencies and instill humility in most leaders. For me, I feel honored when someone listens to my teachings on a subject.

Working on a team means having the opportunity to collaborate. Being humble is about respecting other people's roles in life. Humility offers us an opportunity to do so much more than simply transfer knowledge because it allows us to set an example and influence others to be humble. It also passes on *their* knowledge with a pragmatic and empathetic tone and develops true leadership qualities. When we can humble ourselves to our own greatness, either real or perceived, we gain so much more than positive influence—we gain internal peace.

We can find ourselves in situations where we don't know something, and that can leave us feeling vulnerable to criticism or attack, and even threatened. If we can show others that we are willing to learn through humility, then our humility may be a positive influence that encourages others to do the same.

When we are feeling vulnerable, we must employ empathy for the situation. Therefore, it is vital to choose to be a positive influence for your teams by taking a path of clear communication that leaves arrogance and ego out of the equation. We can share and receive knowledge in a way that empowers both the mentor and the mentee. When we feel empowered through humility and education, we can positively pass that influence on to others.

Conversely, the opposite side of humility is arrogance. As leaders, we can be proud, but pride can lead to overbearing feelings of being better than others (ego). When a leader thinks they are above everyone else in some measured way—whether that be education level, salary, position, or more—there is generally a breakdown in their values of composure and ability to communicate effectively. The ego that stems from the human mind can make even the most humble person think they are above others. When we allow our egos to tell us that we are better than others, we may act differently, affecting our ability to remain composed and communicate positively. Becoming overbearing because of arrogance will derail the best of leaders and topple the best of organizations.

I'll share a short story to give you an example of how arrogance can affect us personally and professionally. One day, there was a new salesperson working at a John Deere dealership. At this dealership, salespeople shared potential leads by taking turns with opportunities, meaning if it was your turn and someone came to the dealership, that person was your opportunity. The new salesperson had an opportunity when an old, beat-up pickup truck drove in. Seeing the old pickup truck and the farmer driving it, the new salesperson decided to offer that opportunity to the next person (feeling as though this opportunity was beneath him). Well, looks can be deceiving. That farmer bought $26 million worth of equipment over the next 18 months.

The tendency to act and feel like we are better than others still exists today in all levels of humanity. Opportunities are lost for those who neglect objectivity and decency and choose to fall back on arrogance. This attitude can derail business relationships as individuals progress up their team's corporate ladder. Don't burn a bridge with anyone unless you have to (which we will touch on later in this book); you never know who someone truly is. As they say, don't judge a book by its cover.

Leaders who forget where they came from, or what it takes to maintain a viable organization, risk being held accountable through loss: Loss of money, respect, stature, position, employees, and perhaps even the business as a whole. When a leader forgets their place and does not employ humility, they chip away at their ability to be a positive influence on the world around them.

One of the best ways to be humble on a team and as a leader is to get in the habit of sharing. What do I mean by sharing? Success in an organization is always a "we," not an "I" effort. A leader who offers recognition to those who do the heavy lifting in an organization shows humility. A leader who takes the time to visit their subordinates at all levels shows humility. A leader who recognizes everyone for their contribution to the successes of the team shows humility.

Being on a team and maintaining humility means accepting successes and failures *together*. Throwing your team under the bus when things go wrong or not including them in the acceptance of an award is not the way to do things. When there are failures, being humble means sharing the consequences with the team. Influential leaders accept the responsibility of failure and commit to working with their team to rectify the failures; when success is achieved, they will give the credit to that same team.

It's not a negative thing to feel proud of yourself for accomplishments. When you become boastful and arrogant, however, you risk diminishing your success as a positive leader. On the other hand, there are some leaders who take humility too far and end up being self-deprecating, undermining their abilities. Confident humility is knowing one's worth without inciting the needs of ego. Being humble doesn't allow for the stroking of one's ego or even make you feel very good at times. It allows you to recognize others and yourself. You must find balance in all things.

By showing humility, it becomes easier to understand your team and anticipate their needs. When we are not caught up in ourselves—how great we are, what we need, or what we are doing—we become a leader who attracts positivity. Our teams will enjoy working with us. Being humble allows us to gauge what our teams truly value in their work environments. When we can pay attention to what our teams need by being humble, their values become clear.

Key Takeaways: Humility

- Ego can get in the way of showing humility. Being humble allows you to stay grounded while remaining mindful of your ego.

- You should feel proud of yourself for accomplishments. It's when you become boastful and arrogant in your pride that you risk diminishing your success as a positive leader.
- If you ever feel that you may be the smartest person in the room, ward off arrogance by taking a mentorship approach to remain humble.
- Humility equals internal peace. The humbler you are, the more aligned with yourself you become.
- Leaders can show humility by offering recognition to those who deserve it, visiting employees at all levels of the organization and getting to know them, and sharing the success of the team with the whole team.

Values

Defining your values, and sticking to them, can prove to be a struggle for us all. Values are the ideas, philosophies, and actions you find most important in your life, including things like compassion, health, family, security, privacy, curiosity, authenticity, and more. However, to be a positive influence on your team, you must do your best to define your values. (If you struggle with where to start, consider visiting the website https://personalvalu.es to discover your core values.) Your values allow you to move forward through life with a kind of compass, and they influence much of how you behave, think, and speak with your teams. They also aid your team in defining what their own values are.

One challenge that can cause some chaos either within us or our teams is the difference in application between personal and professional values. There is a difference, for some, between personal and professional values; however, the issue arises when one behaves inconsistently in either space—meaning, someone is inconsistent in their personal values or their professional values. While these do not always need to overlap, providing consistent behavior helps instill trust in relationships and provides an accurate representation of character. Unfortunately, in the professional world, the justification for going against values is often found in the phrase, "It's just business." In reality, nothing is "just business." It's a cop-out excuse to behave inconsistently for personal gain. Using the phrase, "It's just business" usually means someone is going against their values and using it to avoid feeling potential guilt or possibly to keep trust and character intact when behaving poorly. It means they have set and declared their values and betrayed them for business.

Your values will instill your moral compass (what you believe is right and wrong) and may even extend into how you define what is ethical (the actions carried out by yourself and others that you deem right and wrong). Setting your moral compass means upholding your values at all times—that is the true definition of leadership. Otherwise, you'll be a "Do as I say, not as I do" type of leader, utterly inconsistent and dishonest with yourself and others. To be a great leader, you need to hold onto your values and determine what you are willing to tolerate within your moral compass.

Working on a team means working with individuals who may or may not have the same values you do. However, your values as a *team* should be set by those who are on your team (led by your team's leadership) and defined by your team's goals and desired outcomes. Some of us are lucky enough to work with those who share our same values, while others may be challenged to view the world from another's perspective. If you find yourself on a team lacking *any* values, you will need to determine if there is value in being a team member in that environment.

During my career as a business consultant, I have noticed several shared values of successful, positive teams: trust, stability, kindness, structure, and respect. (I would also like to note that several of the other sections in this book are about values teams hold as well.) There are certainly more, but to discuss all the positive values a team may have could take a book of its own. I want to focus on the five qualities I just mentioned, as they are some of the most basic in a team environment, and they are all positive.

Trust

Trust is something that is generally earned. Trust is the belief that others will be honest, authentic, and reliable. Trust is a value that, I believe, is generally universally accepted. History shows us that trust is the foundation of many relationships, and that hasn't changed to this day. In some situations, trust can take years to earn and be lost in a single moment. However, there are some teams that cultivate such a positive culture that even new employees trust them without it having to be earned.

By working with others, you have already decided to trust them on some level. You may have reservations and may be even more aware of your surroundings when integrating with new people, but you have established a baseline of trust. *How*, you might ask. Well, you generally do some preparation before deciding to work with someone. Your foundation of knowledge is either built on what you read or researched about this person or what you have been told by, most likely, trusted colleagues. This is a building block in the foundation of trust. To build on that foundation of trust, you must apply these three actions: (1) be honest, (2) be transparent and have effective communication, and (3) follow through on what you say you will do. These steps build trust over time. If you follow these three tenets of trust-building, then you can continue to build trust among your teams, even when setbacks occur.

There are always exceptions to the rule. There are differing levels of trust, and trust is not universal. One example of trust-building happens often in business. I have worked with teams that I can and do trust immensely, but not with everything. For example, we have employees I would trust to represent our company in any sales-related function, including managing the sales process from start to finish, but I would not trust them to manage any other type of organizationally challenging process (meaning I wouldn't trust our sales team to manage accounting or change management, for example).

Understanding what motivates someone to be trustworthy and to trust others is key to managing team values. If employees don't value their own work or the work of others, then there are risks of that work not being completed or being done incorrectly. If you find that motivating people to be trustworthy is an issue, you must lead by example by reinforcing the three tenets of trust. When you lead by example and not just words, you display the positive aspects needed to build trust or to help make others trustworthy. You also display another team value: stability.

Stability

Stability, the feeling that something will likely not be disturbed or disrupted, can be measured in several ways; however, much like bricks in a foundation, when key components are missing, it creates instability. Employees may perceive stability as something different than managers, vendors, or customers. Stability is usually subjective to the industry or situations we encounter day to day. Our ability to remain consistent in our words and actions in the presence of external change affects whether others feel secure with us.

It is important for leaders and companies to provide the security that Abraham Maslow's hierarchy of needs spells out:

1. *Food and Shelter*: Food, shelter, and clothing, or the opportunity to pay for these things.
2. *Safety and Security*: Personal security through employment, resources, and health. Providing a clean, positive environment fulfills the security needs of working somewhere safe.
3. *Belonging, Friendship, and Love*: Having a sense of connection to other humans. People want to feel like they are part of something bigger that encompasses more than just themselves; this can be achieved by building personal and professional relationships.
4. *Status, Self-Esteem, and Ego*: Self-esteem, status, recognition, and respect. Individuals hold themselves in a positive regard and they want to be appreciated for their contributions to a team setting.
5. *Self-actualization and Self-fulfillment*: Once the above four levels are met, individuals reach a point where they can focus on being the best they can be. Our goal with this series is to help guide individuals to this last level where we can all be our best selves.

Maslow's theory indicates that each level is dependent upon the previous one, represented as a hierarchal pyramid. Understanding each level and finding a way to provide them to your team will lay a solid foundation and allow individuals to feel stable within the team. Leaders who pay attention to the needs of their team can identify what each individual is lacking in order to reach self-actualization. When your team is at level five, you can empower each person and create stability within their area of influence—which, in turn, creates stability for the team.

One of the best ways to pay attention to the needs of your team is to identify what they are lacking in order to engage them and get to know them. Slow down and pay attention. When you notice their behavior change, make no assumptions about what they need. Instead, ask questions to determine how you may best meet their needs. Ask them if there is anything you can do to help, make a verbal note that you notice they aren't feeling their usual self, and listen and be present for their answer. Additionally, be sure to praise your team often. Identify their (I)individual goals. Create goals or milestones for each person and follow up with positive affirmations to encourage self-actualization.

By providing a stable environment, we create opportunities for our team to feel safe in their ability to self-actualize. Generally, people enjoy having structure, including the structure of having goals, receiving praise, and knowing the limits. Another key aspect of stability is how we treat others, meaning how we treat them when everything is smooth sailing versus when we need to hold them accountable. One of the challenges leaders face is maintaining boundaries while also maintaining stability, holding people accountable, and remaining kind.

Kindness

Being kind doesn't mean we have to be pushovers or look the other way when others violate our values. Kindness means we treat people with respect and identify failure as an opportunity to improve. Some may view kindness as a weakness, but in today's world, I view it as a strength. We are currently facing a time when people are losing the ability to communicate face-to-face with strangers without thinking, "What does this person want from me?"

My wife, René, is an extremely kind person, as many would tell you. She says "hello" and has a warm demeanor toward just about every person she meets. Over the last 20 years, I have witnessed a steady decline in the number of people who reciprocate her friendly advances. This disconnect from personal human interaction—and a potential lack of kindness—is creeping into the culture of organizations around the world. Since you spend nearly a third of your adult life in the company of the people you work with, the culture of that environment is extremely important.

As a leader, being kind is imperative to your company culture and goals. Have you heard the phrase, "You catch more flies with honey than with vinegar"? By being kind to your team, they will be more productive, ready and able to take on the tasks needed so the organization can advance. You can get so much further when you are kind. The same applies for the culture of an organization. When someone enters a place of business and the culture is positive and kind, their sense of wellbeing and comfort adds to their customer experience. How people feel when working with you sticks with them.

Structure

Being kind is something we should all strive for, but, as leaders, we face challenges in acting in a kind way all the time. I have heard leaders struggle with the need for organizational structure and wanting to be kind. By giving our team structure, we are giving them stability. By giving them stability, we are meeting their needs for a safe environment, which is an act of kindness. We can be kind leaders and still demand structure, but only if our communication is positive and open.

Alternatively, chaos gets in the way of people operating functionally. Structure is a foundational tool we have to minimize chaos. Chaotic environments tend to lead to stress, which leads to negative emotions. Chaotic environments are generally reactive, meaning that each situation feels new and perhaps like a surprise, with little to no organization behind what happens next. This then influences our ability to remain kind and objective. People benefit from having structure at home, things like dinnertime or consistent chores; having structure at work will give people those same feelings of belonging and security.

When we combine structure and values, such as kindness, we create opportunities to understand the proper way to complete tasks or deal with issues while sticking to those values. For example, when people know what is expected (structure), they are not surprised, or they are less likely to think something is unkind when it happens or does not happen within that structure. Dealing with peers, customers, and vendors is a good example of this.

One simple example I have of this is setting due dates and being consistent in upholding them; when we set due dates (our expectations that provide structure for which something needs to be completed), we provide our team a kind way of knowing how and when to deliver their finished work product. Without due dates, the tasks may be pushed off or even forgotten, which could cause issues in another area of the company or for other team members who were relying on that work. When due dates are set, accountability for missing the due date can be upheld, and it is less likely that the person will think this accountability is unkind due to the structure provided to them through communicating the desired time at which the product should have been finished.

Respect

Finally, respecting ourselves and others means we value ourselves and others. Respect stems from a place of composure and understanding for our teams. It is something we all intrinsically value; we enjoy being respected and look forward to encountering people we respect. Teams built on a foundation of structure and accountability led by kindness can lead to them receiving respect from their market. Some of our organizations and those of our clients have built respect for themselves by following the values of structure and accountability.

One example I can share includes one of our manufacturing companies. Our company performs educational discussions where we often work shoulder-to-shoulder with our competitors. During one of our educational discussions, an attendee (who was a known advocate of our competition) began heckling our team, voicing his opinions, and becoming argumentative with other attendees. Our reply was to welcome his opinion and express to the other attendees that they were allowed to voice their opinions and be advocates of other products as they saw fit. We respected him and his opinions while not trying to deter him from what he believed. We have continued to build trusting relationships with attendees, peers, competition, and others by sticking to our values.

Adhering to a set of values allows us, as leaders, to control some of the aspects of the challenges we face. Values allow us to utilize and deal with difficult or negative situations that may influence us or our team.

Key Takeaways: Values

- A positive leader sets personal values and doesn't compromise them for business. Using the phrase, "It's just business," is an excuse to betray personal morals for some gain. Leaders who compromise values for business are often inconsistent and dishonest with themselves and others.

- The top values we have noticed consistently across positive teams are: trust, stability, kindness, structure, and respect.
- To build trust, you must be honest, remain transparent, have effective communication, and follow through on your words with promised actions.
- Leaders and companies can provide stability for their teams by understanding Abraham Maslow's hierarchy of needs. Leaders must understand the role they play in this hierarchy, as well as being on the lookout for where their team members are on the hierarchy.
- Kindness is a strength in today's world. Kindness is when you treat others with respect and identify their perceived failures as opportunities for growth.
- You can be a kind leader and still demand structure, but only if your communication is positive and open. Structure can create an environment of security and belonging.
- Respecting yourself and others means you value and understand yourself and others, as well as maintaining an ability to be composed.

Influence Reflection

Being a leader isn't always easy; it's a calling to serve and guide others. Doing your best to be your best is the only way to lead. There is enough negativity in this world as is; your teams all deal with negativity every day. Take it upon yourself to give them a positive leader they can rely on. Having a positive influence in this world is paramount. We are all capable of being a positive influence if we can begin to understand the responsibility that influence entails.

Chapter 2

Understand the Responsibility

"If your actions inspire others to dream more, learn more, do more and become more, you are a leader."
—John Quincy Adams

Everything you say or do not say, and do or do not do, has influence; that's why it is your single greatest responsibility as humans.[1] Every action you take, word you express, and thought you allow to permeate your mind has the power to be influential. That means that, to some degree, we are all role models. Your responsibility is to

1. It's important to note here that we exclude children from this premise, as children under the age of about 15 are primarily developing their influence from those around them. Their peers are being influenced, and they, in turn, influence the children around them.

be the best influence you can in all interactions. That's a lot to handle, right? Well, we want to help you understand this responsibility.

Most of us like to be rewarded. Some of us look forward to being promoted, and some of us may feel that in order to excel at what we do, we need to be rewarded with more responsibility because that means we will make more money. However, when money is the sole purpose for seeking more authority, I wonder if those people truly understand the responsibility that comes from such growth. One of the most misunderstood aspects of leadership is the responsibility that comes with influence.

Some of the most visible people in our society today are "influencers," such as politicians, athletes, actors, and YouTubers. These individuals have a talent that offers them financial rewards and visibility that makes them immediately influential. Their influence extends far beyond the primary role of their position in their field of work. Due to today's technology, and a growing tendency to follow those who have a perceived status of fame or visibility, influencers have a lot of power over their followers.

If you want to be a leader or a positive influence on those around you (and yourself), you must understand the responsibility that comes with your influence. This means understanding the influence you have, what influences you, and how to channel your influence in a positive way. One of the challenges you face growing up from childhood into adulthood, and even growing as a person, is defining your values. How you define your values is how you define your influence.

I am not sure at what age we begin to understand the concept of our influence, but for me, I am reminded of when I was preparing for my discharge from the U.S. Army. I was stationed at Fort Sill, Oklahoma, and I was lucky enough to be assigned to drive for an Airborne officer who was training with the artillery battalions.

He gave me two simple instructions and trusted me to take care of them: 1) Be responsible for myself, meaning that I would continue to attend physical training and keep my room and self squared away. 2) Follow his schedule to a "T." As a reward for completing these tasks, he respected me. He was a Lieutenant Colonel dealing with an enlisted soldier on his way out of the military; he owed me nothing.

I was merely doing what was expected, but he gave me his utmost respect in return. This was a type of respect I had not encountered before, nor had I ever given it. His respect was based on me merely doing what was right. His response had an influence on me that I would not fully understand until later in life, when I began interacting with and comparing my companions from the military with my schoolmates from K-12.

I realized the kind of respect he showed came from those who had been in the military or had grown up in an environment with a structure akin to the military. This realization helped me understand the responsibility leaders have on those they influence; that through the respect given to authority and the structure or chain of command in whatever situation you find yourself in, you can earn respect merely for doing what is right.

The Influence of Leadership

The moment a person becomes a leader is not always clearly defined. However, we are all born influencers. If we can understand, and help others understand, what it means to hold the responsibility of influence early in life, then we can become, or help others become, great leaders and great influencers. Some of my peers see this as a negative; they are afraid that too many leaders means there won't be enough followers. That way of thinking is unproductive and propelled by ego. Furthermore, I don't believe it's true.

Too often, people equate leadership with being "the boss." While I do believe there can be too many *bosses* in one organization, I don't believe there can ever be too many *leaders*. Leadership is not about having control; it's about having influence. When we create leaders, we are attempting to create positive influencers that fill different roles. Leaders can intertwine and work together, but not all leaders are at the top of a company. Leadership is a mindset or way of life based on the influence each of us has.

The culture of shared leadership—where everyone understands the responsibility of their influence and aims to make their thoughts, words, and actions have a positive impact—does not mean that the bosses (or those in charge of making decisions) lack real authority. It also does not mean that there will be too many people trying to run the show. When a company has a traditional organizational structure (understanding of who does what and for/with whom), leaders can work hand-in-hand with the bosses. One issue we often identify with our clients is that their team doesn't feel they have the right to speak up about their opinions or observations of the company. They often feel that they don't have permission to speak their mind if it's not in their area or job description. However, when the bosses are well-defined (structure), but leadership is shared, then all team members can speak freely. This means that the organization has an open-door policy for people to be and feel empowered to share their observations in a structured and respectful way. However, be warned: People who have the attitude that "they are the boss" will have difficulty accepting this kind of leadership culture.

Like me, I am sure most of you would much prefer to be in the company of those who understand their influence and the responsibility that comes with it. A leader does not necessarily always need to have a fancy title. People who aren't at the top of the professional chain can still be positive and influential leaders. Who's to say that your job title defines whether you can lead?

To put this in simpler terms, how often have you been with someone or a group of people who say, "You can choose where we eat tonight" or "Pick what movie we are going to watch"? These are moments when we have the opportunity to make decisions for the entire team, which means we are influencing them. We are the leader of the moment, and we have a responsibility to take that moment and do the best we can with it.

My hope is that by understanding how even small choices have an influence, we can understand how larger, more important choices have exponentially more influence. It's time to prepare ourselves to take on the responsibility of our influence so that we can become positive leaders. To start us off, one of the best (and hardest) ways to learn about our responsibility of influence is through failure.

Failure of Responsibility

Influence can be used irresponsibly and is, therefore, a failure. It does not take much thought to come up with examples: We could dive straight into politics, sports, show business, and more. These are high-profile examples of people who either don't understand their influence or do and choose not to use it wisely. Failure of responsibility can come in many forms, with the following being the most common. First, it can come from knowing you have influence but choosing to ignore it. Second, it can come from not understanding you have influence. Finally, it can come from knowing you have influence and not performing due diligence prior to jumping into something.

When we know we have influence, but choose to ignore it or use it negatively, most of the time, it is because we don't care about what happens to the people on the other side of our influence. This shows a lack of compassion and awareness for the experiences of others, including their suffering. If you know you have influence but act in such a way that you don't care about how you affect others, you are acting without compassion. Acting this way comes from a place of selfishness and ego, which will never allow you to progress as a positive influence. You need to truly consider how your thoughts, words, and actions create a ripple of influence in the world.

When we don't understand we have influence, we cannot rise to the full potential we have to become leaders. However, if someone doesn't know they have influence, we can't entirely blame them simply for being ignorant, can we? How can we control something we don't know we have? For example, at times in our lives, we may feel anxious, depressed, or experience other mental health issues that prevent us from understanding our influence. In these times, it is difficult to lead and control our influence. In addition, when we are growing up, before we reach the point where we understand how we impact the world, we don't recognize that we have influence. There is a time in everyone's life when it just clicks that we have influence, and from that moment on, we must choose to wield our power wisely and responsibly.

When we know we have influence but don't perform due diligence and research the consequences of our actions, we have failed ourselves, our teams, and our ability to influence positively. For example, we may become very excited about an idea to take ourselves or our team in a new direction. Some will just dive right in without considering what that choice leads to, how it will affect them, and how it could affect their team. Without performing research, we may put the cart before the horse and find out later that it is not what we expected. Depending on the path we've chosen, this could end up hurting ourselves or others, which may have been prevented if we had slowed down and done due diligence to understand the consequences of our choice.

Thankfully, there is a flip side to failure that can be turned into a positive. If we understand that we have failed, the best part is that we now have an opportunity to learn and grow from our failure. We can think about strategies and tactics to avoid causing the same failure in the future. However, we must employ tactics of consistency, honesty, and empathy to create an environment that is more objective and provides the balance we need to fully understand our influence. We will discuss these tactics in greater detail later in this chapter.

I recently attended an association conference that, in my opinion, was a failure. This association has a tremendous amount of responsibility due to its influence but has yet to fully realize its full potential. To start, this association has a responsibility in the development and maintenance of standards that protect the general public from injury and possible death. The standards also protect property and the environment from damage. Their standards have been recognized by the American National Standards Institute (ANSI).

Why was this association conference a failure? There was a speaker who has a reputation for being structured and knowledgeable, which leads others to assume he is honest and trustworthy. His topic for the conference was new developments in the industry. He began his presentation with a speech about how he was going to focus on the facts and leave it to the audience to decide their own interpretation of those facts. He then proceeded to deliver a speech laden with opinions and off-handed comments that made it crystal clear that his intention was to influence the audience.

In my opinion, the failure here was regarding the organization, which, when presented with these discrepancies, became aggressive in support of the presenter who was not being honest to the attendees or himself. This type of action isn't limited to just this organization. It plays out, over and over, within the confines of many associations, companies, and wherever groups of people have influence over larger groups. They develop ways to marginalize people or organizations that challenge their way of doing business—thus failing in their responsibility of being leaders.

My example isn't just an exception to the rule. This same person, who has great influence within the organization and industry, has been challenged to be accountable for his poor behavior in the past. He previously expressed aggression toward other members and quit, in writing, the position he held representing the association. However, we later learned that he still represented the association and had zero accountability for his earlier acts and resignation. Power can have a negative effect on certain individuals, and it will contribute to their failure in taking responsibility.

If someone challenges you for something you did and you are unwilling to have a reasonable discussion about it, then you are failing your responsibility. When people see themselves as the foremost expert in a field, they often feel that what they say should be renowned like the gospel. This closed-minded arrogance leads to ultimate failures. In life, we always have the ability to evolve, adapt, and learn. If we don't embrace this fact, or that those around us are experiencing their own change, then we will fail in our responsibility to manage our influence.

Further, by not holding ourselves or others accountable, we also perpetuate failure. If we knowingly allow someone to get away with behavior that we know isn't right, without at least addressing the issue with the offender directly, then we are aiding that person in failing their responsibility while we fail our own. If those actions affect anything within a larger group, we are aiding in that group's failure. By sweeping issues under the rug, organizations fail to positively influence their clients/customers, teams, and other organizations.

These failures aren't limited to work. They can also occur in personal relationships and chance encounters with other people or organizations. One of the most prolific examples I see on a weekly basis is flashing lights at speeding cars to alert them of a police officer ahead so they can avoid getting a ticket. Flashing your lights into oncoming traffic to warn them means you are failing your responsibility as a law-abiding citizen to those who are speeding and to those around you. When you warn speeding people that a cop is ahead, you take away their opportunity to be held accountable for risky behavior. You also fail the people who could be affected by this person's speeding in the future.

I live in a rural neighborhood that is bordered by two suburban towns. There is a main road that connects us all, but my home street is a popular shortcut. There are houses with families, kids, and companion animals, plus a multitude of deer, foxes, raccoons, and other wildlife. The posted speed limit is 25 miles per hour, and on the connecting road, it's 30. I've observed the average speed of people passing through both areas in excess of 45 miles per hour; we have had several animals and one person hit, not to mention all the cars that end up in ditches during the winter.

This is a failure of responsibility. Yes, sometimes it's just speeding, but other times, there are children or animals playing outside. There are posted limits to protect them from speeding cars. When we revoke someone's right to be held accountable, we are allowing them to continue that behavior into the future. We must hold people accountable for their actions today to create a positive influence for tomorrow. Case in point: A few years ago, we had a kid end up in the ditch in our yard due to driving too fast; now, when I see that kid driving by our home years later, he is driving the speed limit.

Additionally, going beyond the failure of holding someone accountable is failing to stop them from doing something that could harm themselves or others (or, doing something we know isn't right). For example, if we allow a friend who has been drinking too much to convince us they are okay to drive themselves home, we become complacent and have responsibility for anything negative that comes from us trusting that friend. Some may feel like this is not their responsibility, but it is. We have responsibilities to our teams, friend groups included. We are a community and absolutely need to look out for each other.

Continuing the example above, if you take improper action, you are still responsible. You may choose not to say something to a friend who has been drinking too much instead of confronting them, but choosing to not act is still an action. By not saying anything to your friend, you are taking improper action. You are not looking out for that person, yourself, or others if you do not abide by what is right. Additionally, you can take action and not understand the context or consequences of that action. Someone who is inebriated can't fully comprehend the consequences of their actions. Jumping to conclusions is another way you can take action and not understand the context or consequences of that action. Assumptions can lead you down the wrong path, as assuming doesn't give you enough concrete information to choose the best path to act.

I am often asked, "Why do we fail?" There are several explanations for why we fail, the most common being that we as humans are inconsistent. Inconsistencies create an imbalance for us and those we influence. Another reason we fail is when we are not honest, either with ourselves or with others. Our communication skills may be imbalanced, meaning we talk more than we listen, or vice versa. If we combine our ability to tolerate inconsistency with an ability to lie to ourselves and justify our or another's actions, we have an equation for failure.

We can always mend our failures, and there are a multitude of ways to do so. We can take a first step toward mending our failure of responsibility by owning that failure and holding ourselves accountable. We can try to engage in activities that will mend the failure or, if we cannot mend it, accept the consequences of our actions. Simply ignoring a failure due to embarrassment or the need to deflect isn't how we grow as leaders. The only way to learn a positive lesson from our mistakes is to own them.

Key Takeaways: Failure of Responsibility

- The three top failures of responsibility are: 1) Knowing you have influence and choosing to ignore it, 2) not understanding that you do have influence, and 3) knowing you have influence but not performing due diligence prior to wielding that influence.
- You must embrace that one of the greatest things in life is the ability to evolve, adapt, and learn from failure.
- You must hold yourself and others accountable. Failure to do so is a failure of positive influence.
- You can fail by being inconsistent and dishonest. These are natural traits that everyone experiences, but you must be mindful to stay true to yourself and your values in order to produce your most positive influence.

Own Your Mistakes

You will make mistakes, and they will have an impact on you and those you influence. The bright and beautiful side of this is that everyone makes them. Mistakes are opportunities for everyone to learn something, and, hopefully, something positive will come from them. While it's true that we all make miscalculations, some of us aren't that great at owning up to them. To be the "I" in team, you must continually work on owning up to these errors. It's part of your self-accountability, but it's much deeper than that. You owe it to yourself, your teams, and your organization to own up to your mistakes and identify their root cause.

The first step to owning a mistake is recognizing that you made one. This can be very difficult for people who are in leadership roles, but all good leaders know how to recognize and own up to their blunders. You may be wondering how to own up to your mistakes and what that process entails. There is always a price to be paid, and that is accountability. However, the price is not always a monetary value. Accountability for an error can range from the internal realization that leads to self-doubt, to the loss of credibility and respect. There is also the loss of money, stature, position, or what I think is most costly of all—loss of a relationship.

I have noticed a pattern: When a person owns up to their mistakes, the consequences can be less severe, and—depending on how the mistake is discovered or communicated—the severity of what needs to be accounted for is reduced. I believe this stems from our ability to feel empathy for those who own up to their role in mistakes. Most individuals have some amount of respect for those who can do this.

Context, as always, matters. If you are owning up to your faults, you shouldn't do so because you believe you will have reduced consequences or accountability. The number one reason to own up is to mitigate any future risks that result directly or indirectly. This is primarily because your mistakes affect more than just your immediate area; there is usually a ripple effect of influence (an influence ripple), like having a vendor who is late with supplies and then delays their clients' products from arriving to their customers on time.

Undoubtedly, it can be scary to admit our miscalculations because admitting this often comes with negative emotions and embarrassment (which, I believe, is why we can empathize with those who choose to do so). We all know what it feels like to have guilt and embarrassment because we made a mistake, so usually, our empathy for others is enough for us to recognize that they have learned their lesson. In some cases, further discipline or consequence is not required.

I want to restate a very important point for this section: You should not own a mistake for the sole purpose of getting out of accountability. Your goal should be to learn and grow, so these issues don't happen again; or if something similar does happen, hopefully, it is less severe. Focus on the positive lessons from making and owning up to a mistake: What lesson did you and your team learn? What value is there to your team for you owning up to your mistake? When you decide to own it, don't rely on justification to minimize the impact of potential consequences because there may be consequences, even when you own up to your error.

To give you an example, the following is how I set up some of our clients for the inevitable oversights my team and I will make. We have a client who has been with us for many years. We provide advisory services to this client as a fractional Chief Operating Officer and Chief Financial Officer, and my primary role is to develop their business strategy for the future. Early in the relationship, when the scope of my personal involvement was identified along with our team's responsibilities, I informed our client that I would likely make some mistakes. The client was visibly flabbergasted. He said, "Why would you tell me that? What kind of mistakes are you referring to?"

My reply was simple, "While I am very good at what I do, because I am human, I will personally make mistakes. Additionally, I cannot control what others do, which includes your team and mine. Because of this, I may make some decisions that rely on others to do certain things. I trust that as a team, we will choose the best people to complete those tasks, but those people will sometimes be inaccurate or miscalculate. I won't blame them, nor will my team; we will accept the responsibility and fix the issues to the best of our abilities to move forward with your goals and our agreement. Again, I tell you this because mistakes are inevitable."

Typically, at first, our clients don't quite know what to say when we discuss mistake mitigation. Although many clients rely on contracts that have consequences built into them if there is a failure, very few openly discuss how their organization handles issues that inevitably occur in the regular course of business (as they do in life). Through the years, we have had some challenges. Clients are rarely happy about the mistakes we've make, but they know when mistakes happen, we will minimize the impact on their businesses. Hence, we have clients we have provided advisory services to for over 27 years, despite some mistakes, and we have expanded their (and our) influence each year to the benefit of their organizations and our team.

Human nature is to deflect, so that is part of our reluctance to discuss slip-ups and how we mitigate them. Accepting direct responsibility for our errors feels wrong—it can sometimes leave us with feelings of guilt and anxiety. Generally, our initial psychological response for taking responsibility for a mistake will be negative, and that immediately leads to defense mechanisms, like our "fight or flight" response to danger. This response can lead us to deflect responsibility, which can include dishonesty about it. Admitting a mistake means we may be held accountable, and, as we have already seen, accountability or the fear of it can make us do the opposite of what a leader should do.

Internal struggles such as these bring us back to some of our previous lessons about self-management. These lessons help to clarify the importance of self-reflection and understanding our internal thoughts, hopefully in a positive way. If you are not secure in who you are as an individual, it may be difficult for you to accept responsibility for things that are under your direct management.

Consequently, it will be virtually impossible for you to accept responsibility for issues under your indirect management. Regardless of who makes a mistake on your team, if you are the leader, you should be able to accept the responsibility for your entire team.

One of our centurion clients (a family business started over 100 years ago) provides an example of an eye-opening lack of accepting responsibility for a mistake that I have ever encountered. The business is local, and in an industry where the public should know its name, especially by the companies who sell its products. René was shopping in a store that sold this client's product, and she happened to be carrying a bag that had the client's logo and tagline printed on the outside. During checkout, the cashier pointed to the bag and mentioned how he and his family would really like to find a product like the one depicted on the bag; to this, René replied that the product was sold right there in that store (to the surprise of the checkout person and his support person).

The day after René shared this story with me, I sent a note to the CEO of the company regarding this encounter. This retail outlet that René was at is very established in our region, and our client has been named their "Vendor of the Year" on numerous occasions. I explained that his company should have better name recognition overall, especially within the ranks of their retail sales partners. We had already had previous discussions about marketing and the best way to create a strong regional and national brand.

Rather than leading to further discussion regarding marketing strategy or brand awareness, this issue was redirected by the CEO to the hiring practices of their retail partner. The CEO's excuse for a lack of brand recognition was not that the company had almost entirely ignored any real budget for marketing for the past 25 years but that the retail outlet staff was not capable of understanding or knowing that his brand was sold at that store. Afterward, we had very little interaction because this company has the same mindset for almost all its issues: It's someone else's fault. You may wonder how a company this size has made it this long with this type of management, to which I would respond that some businesses succeed despite themselves. However, they can never reach their full potential and influence the market as they potentially could.

Owning your mistakes is more than just accepting you have made one. The first step to owning it is to truly accept responsibility, which is different than merely affirming you have made the mistake. There are some people in the world who will say what they think others want to hear in order to get out of accountability for their errors, but that doesn't help them grow their positive influence. Make it known to your team that you are owning the mistake and doing your best to rectify it. That doesn't necessarily mean you must fix all your faux pas on your own; your team is there to help you—but you must lead them. By taking accountability, you can identify and rectify the problem before it is discovered by someone else. Many times, people will hope their mistake is never found out and will attempt to "sweep it under the rug." To be a true positive and influential leader, you can't do this. You must hold yourself accountable and attempt to resolve the issue as efficiently and quickly as possible.

The point of holding yourself accountable isn't so that you or your team can have someone to blame; fixing a mistake isn't about determining who is at fault. Often, teams will focus on trying to figure out who is at fault instead of trying to rectify the issue. Fixing the mistake to the best of your ability should be your only goal. It's not important to focus on "who" prior to solving the issue. There is nothing gained by trying to determine who is at fault before dealing with the issue.

Mitigating a mistake should proceed as follows:

1. What risk(s) did this mistake create?
2. What is the quickest and safest way to mitigate it?
3. Mitigate the risk.
4. Mitigate the mistake.

5. Objectively communicate to all involved and affected.
6. Objectively review the mistake to determine the cause.
7. Develop policies and procedures to prevent similar issues in the future.
8. Include participants in the mitigation, review, and resolution processes.
9. Develop/apply accountability.

There are definitely some mistakes that will not be resolved following this structured process; however, we must determine what risk(s) it poses for us, our team, and our client in order to find the quickest way to resolve it. The focus should not be on who caused the mistake unless or until that information becomes important to the overall resolution. We must accept that to err is to be human. Nobody is perfect. When and if we work together as a team to mitigate the mistake and risks, then we can continue to grow our whole team in their Individual positive influence.

By owning our mistakes consistently, we show our team what kind of leader we are. We make them feel secure in knowing that we recognize our failures and work to rectify them. Without recognizing our failures, we leave our teams to scramble with dread and anxiety while they try to pick up the pieces. The fact is, we all fail; it's how we choose to move forward with our teams that define us as leaders. If we can remain consistent when dealing with our mistakes and those of our team, we can establish a positive work culture.

Key Takeaways: Own Your Mistakes

- Owning up to your mistakes means taking the time to understand their root cause. Otherwise, you may cause the same issue again.
- In some cases, owning up to your mistake is enough accountability, and no further discipline or consequence is required. This is because it takes courage to own up to your errors, and

we can all empathize with the emotions that come with this type of honesty.

- When a mistake has been identified, don't immediately search for who caused it. The most important part is rectifying it, mitigating it, and getting everyone back on a positive path. Then, you can work to help the person who made the mistake grow from it.
- **Mitigating a mistake should proceed as follows:**
    1. What risk(s) did this mistake create?
    2. What is the quickest and safest way to mitigate it?
    3. Mitigate the risk.
    4. Mitigate the mistake.
    5. Objectively communicate to all involved and affected.
    6. Objectively review the mistake to determine the cause.
    7. Develop policies and procedures to prevent similar issues in the future.
    8. Include participants in the mitigation, review, and resolution processes.
    9. Develop/apply accountability.

Consistency: The Broken Record

Positive influence requires consistency to have its full impact. Consistency is when you repeatedly tackle an issue, task, or other in the same way so everyone around you knows what kind of response to expect. Most humans don't consciously focus on being consistent. Instead, many may rely on what we like to call "comfortable focus" (or autopilot) to keep them on their path. However, one thing I learned while writing my thesis for my master's degree in information management is that singular individuals can have up to six different responses or actions to the same issue or challenge. Learning this stunned me. What does that mean? That humans are consistently inconsistent?

Being inconsistent does not denote that you are doing bad things. It just means that you have adapted your actions to fit the particular situation. That situation includes current events, your emotions, and the people you may be interfacing with (who are also affected by their own perception of the situation and the emotions that follow). Hypothetically, you could be faced with the exact same situation many times, but depending on your perception of the situation at that time, your reaction falls across a spectrum.

One of the reasons for this is that you're not the same person you were a moment ago. You are constantly learning, changing, and adapting to life. These changes influence your perception and who you are, including how you think and act. If you were faced with the exact same situation at different ages, your life experience at that moment could lead you to respond differently. Similarly, if you were faced with the same situation while in different emotional states, your emotions could influence how you respond. These two examples alone provide a spectrum of responses. However, there are far more things at play that contribute to how you respond to a situation at a particular moment.

Therefore, achieving consistency requires focus, patience, training, and living in the present. Being pragmatic and objective are keys to being consistent. I have come across many people who believe a pragmatic and objective approach to human issues is cold or lacks necessary emotion, but I disagree. It is my belief that if you use pragmatism and remain consistently in the present, you can share your emotions with more freedom. This leads you to wield empathy and other caring emotions more effectively.

Another key to consistency is positive thinking. If you believe in what you do, at all times, you will perform with consistency. You may be confronted with challenges that you don't believe in but feel obligated to do, which can lead you to face them inconsistently. A good example of this comes from one of our clients who sold a Christian board game for children. The team I had originally assembled to work with this client was chosen for their expertise in the area the client needed. However, the team struggled to create content for the client due to religious conflicts. Due to the difference in religious preference, my team hit barriers often and became inconsistent in their creative thought process. Therefore, they were faced with a challenge, but they were obligated to perform their jobs. Ultimately, we had to add team members that could bridge the differences and add context where needed to maintain clarity and consistency. When you face challenges in an inconsistent way, you risk not completely resolving those challenges. These may be viewed as life lessons, but they aren't really lessons if you keep repeating the same thing over and over again with consistently negative results. This is where positivity comes in.

Yet I find it difficult to remain positive all the time. In my life, positivity is challenging because my job is working with clients to resolve negative issues. When you are surrounded by negativity, remaining positive will be a drain on your tank of willpower. You need to develop tools or habits to support positive thinking. One of the best ways I have found to remain positive is journaling my thoughts. There are times when my thoughts can be very negative and venture into places that are dark or even irrational. One good way to manage negative thoughts is to write them down and challenge them.

The act of challenging your own thoughts, when done consistently, will help you defeat negative thinking. You can challenge your negative thoughts by asking yourself a few questions: *Are these thoughts true? Where do these thoughts stem from? Why did I have that thought? What is the opposite of that thought?* If you fail to challenge your negative thoughts (whether they are prompted by you or not), they can manifest in your physical life. If you think positively, you will live positively. This is a simple law of attraction. By being consistent and challenging your negative or untrue thoughts, you will begin to see a decline in those thoughts. Finding the tools to help you battle negativity is one of the keys to the success of your consistency.

One note here about journaling: Make sure the place where you journal these negative thoughts is secure from anyone who may be negatively affected by your writing. I have experienced first-hand what can happen when someone accidentally reads your journal containing private thoughts meant to rid your mind of insecurities, fears, and demons. It can be difficult to remember to secure your personal notes, as they are typically written in an emotional state, but it's vital to slow down to keep your private thoughts private.

Slowing down, a lesson from our first book, happens to be one of the most difficult lessons to learn. However, slowing down is another key component to remaining consistent. When you can slow yourself down, it is easy to remember how to be consistently yourself. Slowing down requires having control over your emotions, thoughts, and actions. By controlling these three things, you will inherently act in a more consistent way.

We need tools to support us in being consistent. Sometimes, it's just as simple as having standards and using policies and procedures to guide us. Standards come in many forms. They can be disguised as laws, regulations, task lists, policies, procedures, and more. However, these tools all serve one purpose in the end: consistency. When we set standards for ourselves, we create a tool that supports our efforts to be consistent. These tools help us stay on track to achieve our goals.

To give you an example, let's look at something many of us encounter in our personal lives: Franchises. Companies like McDonald's, Burger King, Jiffy Lube, and Marriott, to name a few, all use standards to ensure that when you visit any of their locations—in different cities, states, or countries—you have a consistent experience every time. When you don't have a pleasant time in a particular location, that is often because a standard was not met. Additionally, professions like accountants, lawyers, plumbers, and electricians employ industry standards to guide them. Sometimes those standards are universal, and other times, they are more specific to an area or region due to nuances in infrastructure or how the laws are written. Regardless of variances, everyone within these professions follows a set of foundational standards. Thus, these standards create consistency within brands and professions and everything in between.

One of the most frequent and condemning issues in business is a lack of consistency. Many leaders today don't take the time to fully understand what their staff is doing to support the organization. Team members are often left to their own perceived expertise to pick and choose how they address issues. This type of leadership creates chaos and disrupts business. Leaders should rely on their staff to get their work done. However, it should not be to the detriment of the business. Leaders need to engage their team from their 30,000-foot view and provide oversight. They should listen to the input of their team and lead accordingly.

Consistency is something that touches all aspects of business and life. Leaders should not only work on consistency of thought in a way that promotes positivity and progress; they should work on it throughout the organization. Teams that are consistent make progress in a way that generally develops long-lasting results.

One issue that can arise is that, like their leaders, teams are often so focused on their own task that they lack a complete understanding of how their work affects those around them. This is where an inconsistency begins to compound the overall operations of a company. This same inconsistency can affect the culture of the entire team, creating organizational issues within the workplace.

We have had clients who, to this day, are inconsistent throughout their lives. They don't plan for much, meaning they take whatever life throws at them. These clients tend to have a lot of peaks and valleys in different aspects of their lives, including their finances. A good reputation at one time, a tainted reputation at another. A stress-free environment, then a stressful one.

This cycle is the only thing that is consistent in these clients' worlds, meaning that the only consistency is their inconsistency. When and if we can identify that we have a cyclical tendency to be inconsistent, this is a good time to reflect on what is causing us to lose our consistency. What is driving us?

Leaders who are confident and consistent with their standards, policies, and procedures can help their teams stay focused by being a "broken record." To repeat yourself over and over may seem silly to some, but when you give the same answer to the same or similar questions, you are being consistent. You may have to adapt your delivery, for instance, if you are being asked the same question over and over because your team doesn't understand the answer. When your team understands your answer, the team will be led toward a more positive and consistent environment.

When we attempt to get to the root cause of our inconsistency, I believe most of us will find some level of imbalance. We are often imbalanced as we attempt to make a good thing better, or when we attempt to accelerate ourselves past our current position. This throws our life out of balance and causes actions that can end up making us inconsistent. Which begs the question: How do we remain balanced and therefore consistent?

Key Takeaways: Consistency: The Broken Record

- The keys to being consistent are: Focus, patience, training, living in the present moment, being pragmatic, and being objective.
- You can have many different responses or actions to the same issue or challenge. This is because you are constantly changing and reacting to different stimuli in your environment.
- You can battle negative thinking and intrusive thoughts by challenging them consistently. If you do so (consistently), those thoughts will lessen.

Balance

In order for us to continue to have a positive influence, we need to have balance in all areas of our lives, including with our work, leisure, family, or friend time. Without balance, it is very difficult to have consistency. Now, "work/life balance" is one of those buzz phrases that is thrown around casually, often by people who really don't understand what it means because it is so subjective to each of us. While it *is* subjective, I want to take a moment to offer a loose definition for the purpose of this section for clarity.

Generally, work/life balance refers to maintaining balance between how you support yourself financially and the rest of your life outside of work. For some, the work part looks like having a single career where you go to work for eight or more hours per day; for others, it may be multiple jobs, a part-time job, school, or something else. The other side, the life side, could entail spending time with family, friends, or with yourself. It can also involve investing in a hobby or a lifestyle. The point here is that the work/life balance is subjective, as I mentioned earlier, so how you balance yourself will look different from the person next to you. Some may enjoy working more, while others may need to spend more time with their families. The balance comes from within, and it's up to you to determine if you are leading a life of balance.

The problem with the fact that work/life balance is subjective is that sometimes we fail ourselves by creating imbalances we cannot see. I believe this stems from looking at the work/life balance of others and assuming their work/life balance structure is how our balance should look. This can cause an imbalance because what works for someone else may not work for us. To have a proper work/life balance, we might consider asking those we care about how they feel about our current work/life balance.

I have experienced work/life imbalance prior to being in the position I am now. However, in my current position, I rarely think of what I do as work. But there were times in my life when I lacked balance because I focused solely on "the grind" and lost sight of other important things to spend my energy on. I previously discussed the loss of friends and business partners, but those losses are not limited to my professional life. Early in my marriage with René, we had a group of friends who were "above our station." I wrote about them in the beginning of Chapter 7 in *Individual Influence*. They were the ones who pointed out that we were clearly "no Rockefellers."

Another man I thoroughly enjoyed being friends with was an eclectic computer programmer with a good personality; plus, he was fun to be around. He dated several beautiful women, many of whom were successful models in the Denver area; he was a bit shallow when it came to women, meaning he never truly had a meaningful intimate relationship, at least while we were friends.

Regardless of his choices, he was a true friend and treated René and me like equals while we were attempting to climb the socio-economic ladder. He was very into his work and making money to benefit his lifestyle—not in a snobby way. Then one day, he met this amazing woman who shared several of his values. He seemed head over heels for her, and she humbled him a little, which brought out a different side of him. This new relationship had a positive influence on him.

The first thing I noticed was that it slowed him down. He began to be more thoughtful about how he spent his time. In the past, we would meet at restaurants or other upscale locations downtown, but now he would invite us over for a more intimate gathering at his home. However, the rest of our social group did not slow down.

Then one day, he told all of us, "You're just not good friends. You've lost your balance in life." And none of us ever heard from him again. At this time, I didn't understand what a work/life balance was, and I'm sure the rest of the group didn't either, so we just looked at each other like, *What is his problem*? The fact was he had found more balance in his life, and we had not, so he could not maintain his relationship with us. He re-prioritized his life, which meant he wanted people with the same priorities and balance that he discovered.

The rest of us *thought* we had balance. I was building a business and could not see that my life was out of balance. Sure, I worked a lot, but I had a nice home and a beautiful wife and daughter; things seemed great. The future would prove to me that this perception was incorrect. Over the next couple years, what was left of the friend group continued to focus intensely on our careers, so the energy we invested in our families began to decline to keep up our work so we could provide for all the superficial things our social group yearned for. Our focus on building our careers would eventually prove to be less important as our families began to break down; we lost one couple who found their work/life balance, another was experiencing marital issues caused by an imbalanced life, and the rest of us were facing health issues, marital issues, financial issues, or other family issues. All these issues were caused by work/life imbalance.

During this time, I began to understand the meaning of a work/life balance. I think I reached the peak of my imbalance in 2004. My health was not so good for a 38-year-old. I had just come through some difficult partnership issues, which I caused, and those issues put pressure on me to work harder to maintain the lifestyle I thought was needed to keep my family happy. I began a travel campaign that saw me on the road 5 to 6 days a week; oftentimes, I was gone for weeks at a time. I was traveling to the East Coast, then the West Coast, and even over to Hawaii and everywhere in between. Eventually, I was traveling out of the country—all to further my company's efforts.

While the workload was feverish, there was no gig I would turn down, as long as I could be a consultant helping businesses improve. We can never fully anticipate the imbalance created by our decisions; however, we must do our best to stay ahead and imagine the possible outcomes of our actions. Many of our biggest mistakes are the unintended consequences we create in our effort to do good; they are almost never foreseen or thought of until they have an influence on us. As you can surmise, this led to an immense amount of work/life imbalance.

During my, and my family's, search for balance, we overcompensated for one imbalance, which created another. It was in this cyclical effort that I began to ask myself, "Does life need to be this teeter-totter between imbalances, or can we truly find balance in our lives?" To be a positive influence, we must understand not only the imbalances in our own lives but those in the lives around us.

Much of my time as a business consultant is spent balancing my clients' organizations, their lives, or both. Several of the tools I have developed over the years have been focused on understanding the balance/imbalance within an organization. Balance in an organization is not solely focused on the number of employees doing one thing or another, just as the balance we have personally is not solely focused on work, leisure, family, or friend time. The scale of life is not two-sided; it's just not that simple. It's a system in which imbalance in one area causes imbalance in other areas. People who are truly positive influences know this, perhaps subconsciously, and through their subconscious, they act in a way that promotes such balance.

To a certain extent, we need to understand who we are and why we do the things we do. Having this personal understanding of ourselves means that we can become better equipped to realize when we are balanced or imbalanced. We need to face the lies we tell ourselves, and we need to accept that those lies have consequences. Having a positive influence relies heavily on knowing ourselves, which is why our first book focuses on self-reflection and discovery.

Managing and focusing on balancing our lives can sometimes feel overwhelming. This is where our values and understanding of composure come into play—how we justify our choices, our approach toward accountability, and how humble we are. When we have a clear understanding of these aspects of our lives, our ability to control our balance becomes clearer. While we may continue to teeter-totter through this balancing act we call life, we can at least do so with our eyes and minds in the correct place.

Balance at Work

One of the best ways to maintain balance in an organization is to try to instill in everyone that you are all peers working together in the same environment. What one of you doesn't do, another must. Cultivating a true team culture will help to bring balance to everyone and alleviate some of the negative consequences of imbalance, like taking others for granted, laziness, and absenteeism. Does this mean there is not a hierarchal structure in your organization? Absolutely not; it means that any person can correct an imbalance in the organization at any time, which will hopefully keep us all moving forward toward the same goal.

Each team member is responsible for the viability of the company, from the receptionist to the CEO. Your mission should be to fulfill the goals of the company. For example, if you are working and you notice something is counterproductive to the mission of the company and you ignore it, you are creating potential risks.

Alternatively, you can identify the issues right away, share your observation with someone who has the influence to address it, and keep your team moving in a positive direction toward shared goals. The integrity of an organization isn't threatened when one or more individuals break the rules; it is threatened when you decide to do nothing about it. This is where accountability to yourself and your team comes in.

The better foundation we can build for our team and our company, the easier it will be to keep balance. This includes keeping the whole team empowered to speak up for what is right, maintaining the values that are important to them, and holding every member accountable by being consistent. Empowerment is not the only place where balance is important; we must maintain organizational structure as well.

Imbalance in a business can mean many things. For example, maybe there is too much reliance on third parties to accomplish tasks. Maybe a company turns and looks the other way when harassment is present in the workplace, or they cripple their culture in some other way to maintain the status quo. Or perhaps, ownership is taking too much money to provide for their lifestyle. Two of the largest perpetrators of imbalance in business are a lack of sales performance and the inability to fulfill promises or obligations. The first can also be a market issue, where blame cannot be placed solely on the company but on the lack of the market wanting that product or service. Until you know what is causing this imbalance, you can't fix it. The issue of balance is rarely what the client thinks it is.

The second can be better explained by the following scenario. Imagine someone is a great plumber—they're efficient and offer competitive prices. Now imagine that they decide to grow their company, so they solicit another company to build them a website and create a marketing message to increase their exposure.

The company hired to design the website and create a marketing message does exactly what is asked of them. At first, the plumber is happy as their opportunities for business increase. Their knowledge of the industry, the local market, and their affable personality—not to mention their attention to detail—quickly win them new work and positive influence. The business grows, so much so that the plumber realizes they must hire a new plumber to help keep up with the booming business. However, the plumber hired is as technically sound as the owner but lacks the affable personality that won over the client base.

As the company continues to grow in visibility, the owner (the original plumber) must spend more time meeting new people since the new plumber isn't the type to meet, greet, and sell to new customers. Therefore, the owner spends an increasing amount of time chasing new opportunities and leaves the technical work to the new plumber. However, the excited and kind comments the company was receiving prior to the new plumber being hired begin to wane.

In fact, some of the statements are even replaced with off-putting feedback about time delays and lack of personality.

Sales begin to decrease, and even though more plumbers have been hired along the way, as well as a bookkeeper, there are new issues with cash flow and the quality of service that came with the owner's affable personality. The owner then turns to the marketing company who spiked their sales in the past, hoping in a last-ditch effort to help their company regain its traction. However, the company eventually fails because it does not have a balanced foundation between marketing, sales, operations, and administration. How could the owner possibly know it was his personality that made the clients love the company?

Imbalance is the cause of most business failures, and that is what we first identify when my company goes into an organization. Some of the most severe financial decisions are made to maintain an imbalance between what a company can support and the owner's livelihood (which, again, leads to a high rate of small business failure). Your responsibility of influence as the leader of your company, division, department, family, and self is not to put you or those who rely on you at risk. When you live a life of imbalance, you create inevitable risk for others.

As with most things, achieving balance starts with being honest. You may have a skewed perception of the imbalance in your life. It's important to include your team in your effort to re-balance your life, as they can shed light on perspectives that you might not have considered. When you have this open communication about imbalances in your life as a tool to gain more information, you must be honest with yourself about what you learn. Don't dismiss claims if they don't align with what you want—sometimes what you want isn't what you need. Discovering what you need to become balanced begins with being honest.

Key Takeaways: Balance

- Balance is subjective and based on your individual needs and goals. You must determine for yourself how to balance your work and life. Don't chase someone else's life; this will cause imbalance.
- If you know and understand yourself, you can determine what makes you feel balanced and imbalanced.
- To create a balanced work environment, you should instill a culture of understanding that you are a team. What one doesn't do, another must. When one fails, everyone fails. When one succeeds, everyone succeeds.

Honesty

Lying is an ethical discussion that has been ongoing for centuries and has its own influence on our lives. We tend to fail at proactively comprehending the consequences of our lies. Understanding the value and consequences of lying will aid us in uncovering why we lie almost daily, both to ourselves and to others.

We all lie on a regular basis, but not all lies carry the same weight. First, not all lies are meant to harm another person. *Psychology Today*[2] states, "We are interested in truth and lies in people's everyday communication. Most people think a lie occurs any time you intentionally try to mislead someone. Some lies are big while others are small; some are completely false statements, and others are truths with a few essential details made up or left out. Some lies are obvious, and some are very subtle. Some lies are told for a good reason. Some lies are selfish; other lies protect others."

2. Saad, Gad. "How Often Do People Lie in Their Daily Lives?" *Psychology Today*, Sussex Publishers, 30 Nov. 2011, www.psychologytoday.com/us/blog/homo-consumericus/201111/how-often-do-people-lie-in-their-daily-lives

The average lie is typically a white lie. For example, when a spouse asks their partner, "Do I look good in this outfit?" and the other replies "yes" when, in fact, they do *not* like how their spouse looks, this is a white lie. Why do we do this? Isn't the point of asking to receive an honest reply and not to be supported? This is where white lies become tricky, and we each justify them in our own way.

Some individuals ask because they want to know the truth and others ask because they want affirmation. On the flip side, being honest depends on who you want to be and how you want to be perceived. Do you want people to come to you knowing that you will always give them an honest answer, no matter how brutal? Or do you want to be the kind of person that people come to when they need validation or support? Navigating these fine lines takes trial and error. I implore you to decide who you want to be first and then go from there.

Understanding the value and consequences of honesty will help us to understand why we lie. When a person is honest, there is still a chance for consequences. People lie to escape the consequence of the truth or to make an easier path for themselves. In this regard, I think of our flight or fight response—the lie is the flight, and the truth is the fight.

Humans can be impulsive when we fear the consequences of being honest. During our moment of truth, sometimes the thought of the consequences overrides reason, and, as intelligent creatures, we believe we can talk our way out of a situation (often using lies). From my experiences raising three children to my retrospective review of my life and my work with thousands of people and organizations, I have been faced with many people who lie, including myself. The fact is that most lies are inconsequential (white lies). While I don't believe we should fret over white lies, I do believe we must be mindful and strive to always be honest in matters of consequence or influence. As stated previously, we must decide who we want to be and who we want to be seen as.

Allow me to digress to a quick, personal example about honesty. I had always been interested in becoming an accountant, so I lied about my level of knowledge of accounting to gain entry into classes and positions where I could work more with numbers. I had several jobs between 1984 and 1988, and all of them but one was the result of a lie. One job I took was with a copier company in California as a sales administration assistant; my job was to account for the inventory and make sure the small sales office was clean and stocked properly. I embellished my experience with inventories and accounting. I also took jobs as a carpet salesperson, insurance salesperson, and wholesale car sales auditor, all by embellishing my credentials for the positions. Each position was taken to support my aspirations to make as much money and gain as much experience in the shortest amount of time possible.

Embellishment is lying. It's not bending the truth, or even "my truth," it's flat-out lying. There are certainly circumstances and perceptions that you can claim, but that doesn't mean the truth isn't the truth. The consequences of my embellishments were generally stress and embarrassment. I felt embarrassed when I couldn't perform or answer questions that someone of my "caliber" (meaning, someone I said I was) would know. I made easy mistakes and used more lies and embellishment to get my way around them. When I was tired of lying and keeping one story straight with one company, I would move on to the next. I learned the cost of this along the way. It was mostly personal, as the embarrassment I felt was the primary reason I knew I wanted to change. I also lost relationships; people called me out on my lies, and I became tired of defending myself with even more lies. I learned that the more you lie at the beginning, the more you have to lie to keep that thing going. That is *exhausting*.

Thinking back on my early life years has clarified for me the value of honesty from the perspective of influence. By this, I mean that I better understand the cost of dishonesty. Lying means we influence others and ourselves in a negative way, and lies usually come with a cost (like loss of relationships or jobs). Lies damage our reputation, and when we lie on behalf of a company or group, then, by extension, the reputation of our teams and company is damaged as well. If we feel the need to lie about something, we must pay the cost. Therefore, if there is such a cost, it's probably an important factor in your reputation.

Lying will tarnish your reputation, and anyone tied to that reputation, for as long as people remember the lie. If you lie enough to others, you will surely begin to lie to yourself—and believe it. Lying to yourself is sometimes even more dangerous than lying to others, as it can create a false perception of the world that, in your mind, seems true. Being honest protects you and allows you to have a positive influence on yourself and others.

Similarly, the truth can and will hurt people. At times you may feel it's best to "gloss over" the truth to ease people into issues without the full context in the hopes of protecting them. If you are giving people information or telling stories out of context while purposely leaving out pivotal points of information, then you are lying. The truth should not be about context. When you are faced with a challenge like this, how you deal with that situation may define you.

Where does our obligation to be honest end? Well, that is for you to decide. I will remind you that being the "I" in team is still about making a personal choice and having the freedom to control your influence. However, to be your best self—your most positive and influential self—your obligation to be honest never ends. Are white lies that make someone feel good but don't necessarily alter the outcome of any serious situation acceptable? That depends on who you want to be.

If your job, or even if your entire work team, relies on lying and cheating to get by, then you are absolutely part of that conspiracy to lie and cheat. If you don't actively participate in the lying and cheating and claim that you don't, then that is also a lie—the fact that you know and don't do anything about it is your participation.

Should the company ever be held accountable for its actions, you can be included in that accountability, beyond just losing your job.

Knowing that people lie and covering for them is a common issue all humans face. It's also one of the most stressful because that person's lie has put us in a precarious position. This goes beyond being a moral or loyal dilemma and can venture into the legal realm. Common issues like this could be cheating on taxes or other business-related issues.

Honesty is something that each of us struggle with at different times in our lives. The fear of consequence of honesty is generally why we tell remarkable lies. Lying can and will tarnish the value of positive influence. If we lie often, people will uncover the lies and the pattern of lying. The best we can do is be honest, or at least try to be honest, and if we choose to lie and are caught, we must face the consequences.

If you're like most people, there is usually a little voice in your head telling you to do the right thing and be honest. When you fear the consequence of telling the truth, sometimes that voice can get quieter, but it is always there if you choose to listen. In the end, honesty is always the best policy. Listening to your inner voice—the one that tells you to do what is right—is a step toward being a positive leader. Your listening skills, whether listening to yourself or others, are what allow you to make educated decisions if you know how to listen correctly.

Key Takeaways: Honesty

- When determining your level of honesty, consider what kind of person you want to be. Do you want to be someone who validates and supports others no matter what, or someone who will always give an honest opinion? Could you balance both?

- Lies always come with a cost; whether it be friendship, money, or something else, there is always a downfall to being dishonest, even if it doesn't appear immediately.
- If you know that someone else is lying or cheating and you don't say anything, you become an accomplice to that act.

Listening

Knowing how to listen to ourselves, others, and our surroundings may be the most powerful tool we have to be a positive influence on our teams. To take it a step further, the act of "productive listening" is influential on its own. Productive listening is when all parties involved notice and acknowledge, even just to themselves, the attention of the other parties. We practice productive listening by being so intent on listening to the speaker that they *know* we are listening. The perception of being listened to can and will influence the speaker to communicate more thoroughly. For example, when we're talking to someone who then decides to bring out their phone to check something, this would be unproductive listening. After we notice them disengage from the conversation, we may also disengage, leading us to not be as thorough of a speaker.

Listening is more than an act; it is an art. The entirety of listening is a combination of how we listen to others and how we understand our opinion or reaction to that listening. Thinking and understanding our own voice is a method of listening and can often be more important than how we listen to others. How we listen to and make sense of ourselves helps us to comprehend what's happening in our own minds. Our minds can convince us to do and say things that can either damage or enhance our influence, so how we act upon and listen to ourselves is crucial to the state of our influence.

I listen for a living. As an advisor, I need to understand the issues my clients are facing. Most of the time, the issues involve more than one person, so I have to listen to information from multiple sources to gain better knowledge of the issues. It is through listening that I gain these individuals' perceptions of their environment and people they deal with on a regular basis. Moreover, listening allows me to create the foundation of our work.

As I interview and observe, my mind speaks to me. Tapping into my past experiences, I can hear my mind say that I know what the issues are, what the solutions are, and what I should be saying at that moment to begin making the changes needed to assist my client. It is here that I need to listen to myself *while* I listen to my client. My experience wants me to begin fueling my reaction, but I also know that no two issues are ever the same; I must finish listening to the full context before I construct ideas to remedy the issue.

Our impulse to speak and not listen can be fueled by an infinite number of things: Social, emotional, and psychological reasons that, for each of us, are different. To give you some examples, you may feel the need to speak in social settings if you have the gift of gab or are intimidated by the lull in a conversation, perhaps feeling anxious (an emotional need to speak) if nobody else is talking. Other emotional examples could include being so wrapped up in what is going on in your own life that it is difficult to care or listen to others. Sometimes you can't get thoughts out of your head without speaking them aloud to someone else, known as venting. Then, there are some psychological reasons why people feel compelled to converse; some people are just talkers, and their brains go through ideas faster than others, so their ability to slow down and listen could be impaired if they haven't made it a habit. The act of listening will take work and patience with yourself as you navigate the impulse to speak. How often have you been so excited to speak that you cut the other person off before they were finished? Indeed, sometimes the impulse and need to talk can be as powerful as an addiction to drugs.

I don't know about you, but as I mentioned above, cutting others off before they are done speaking is a challenge I have personally faced and worked on for many years. First, when we cut someone off while they are still talking, it robs us of our opportunity to learn more of the context from that person. The simple act of not listening can carry a tremendous amount of risk. Oftentimes, part of the reason we cut people off is because we aren't fully engaged and listening to what they have to say; the other part could be impulse or ego.

Time and experience have shown me that listening pays dividends. It's like putting money in the bank and earning interest. By listening, we can gain knowledge from the experience. We also teach ourselves patience as we practice listening, another trait that will serve us well and improve our influence. As you can see, being a good listener has tremendous value.

The more we listen, the more knowledge we can acquire. The more knowledge we acquire, the more direct and precise we can become in our interactions with others. Instead of talking in circles to get others to understand the point we are trying to make, we can speak more directly about the topic. By slowing down and listening to those around us, we can formulate a way to speak so that we are understood by everyone in our immediate areas of influence.

One of the best ways that speaking can aid in listening is through asking questions. Asking thoughtful and open-ended questions is a huge part of listening, as it shows that you are trying to gather more context from what has already been said. Furthermore, by engaging in listening and asking for more context, you build trust with the other person as they feel they are being heard. If you are listening—truly listening—there will be at least one point that you feel should be clarified, expanded, or explained. Asking questions can also reveal your current knowledge on the topic.

If someone assumes you have previous knowledge on the topic, and you don't, they may leave out key details pertinent to understanding that discussion. Once you begin asking questions, you display your knowledge base, and, if they are listening to you, they will be able to work with you to navigate the topic more easily. It can also help them slow down, which will lead to a more thoughtful and meaningful interaction. When you listen and ask thoughtful questions to pursue context, you lay a foundation of understanding with others. It can also lead to new and profound insights that would not have been unearthed had you not asked questions or been in active dialogue.

By observing and listening to someone speak and communicate with others, you learn how that person understands communication. You can gauge their level of knowledge on the topic, as well as the amount of respect they have for the audience. You can observe tone, inflection, and body language—all of which are a part of listening. You'll have to take note of what your own view of the speaker is as well. Noting how your thoughts and emotions are influenced by the words being spoken are important factors in the listening process. While you want to gauge how others are responding to the speaker, your response is just as important. Your response to how others communicate will tell you a lot about yourself, and you may not always like what you learn.

In the modern world, listening can be performed through reading as we text, email, instant message, tweet, and more. We should listen during all the communications in our lives, including the digital ones. Part of the issue with digital communication is that we lose a lot of the context needed for proper listening: inflection, tone, and body language. We read messages in our minds with our voice, and not in the voice of the person who sent it. Based on our point of view, a neutral text can turn negative if we would have sent the same text with an emoji. Again, the best way to overcome these negative feelings is to ask for context.

There have certainly been moments in our lives when we have been listening to someone and not believed a word they were saying. Usually when we hear something we don't believe to be correct, we have an internal emotional response that can sometimes result in our mouth overriding our listening. How we listen to and understand these internal responses will provide us some context and routes to be observed to learn about ourselves. This all requires us to slow down.

On one hand, we may be hearing the truth, which would mean that the basis for not believing the person is based on opinion or misinformation. On the other hand, we could be correct, which would mean we are presented with a unique opportunity to discuss what each person believes—which, unfortunately, can turn quite ugly in today's world as we have become less and less tolerant of those who have opposing views. We dismiss much of what we hear before we really hear it.

Many of us suffer from confirmation bias.[3] I am not here to say that I or anyone I know is above this phenomenon, but what matters is how we do our best to proceed with a positive influence. We each have favorite sources of getting information, and even the best, most objective sources get it wrong sometimes. I do believe, however, that each of us is influential, and if we wish to use our influence in a positive way, we have a responsibility to listen to those who don't agree with us. It's always possible that both sides are correct—it just depends on the perspective you are looking from. To be a positive influence, we must try to have an objective understanding of those who don't have the same opinions as us.

It's easy to understand that people don't like to admit when they are wrong. It doesn't feel good to be wrong, especially if our belief is rooted in emotions or values. When we take the time to care and listen properly while asking thoughtful questions, we can begin to see a decline in emotional-based issues and an increase in fact-based debates. As an example, with permission from my vegan daughter, Mary, I want to dive into the contested topic of vegans.

Veganism is a great topic for having a thoughtful reflection about how individual positions centered around veganism, plant-based diets, pescatarians, vegetarians, and omnivores can spiral out

3. Confirmation bias is the tendency to look for, interpret, favor, or recall information that confirms or strengthens prior personal beliefs or values.

of control, creating horrible destructive stereotypes and making people lose their sense of humor at the same time. I, personally, choose not to lead a plant-based lifestyle. Being plant-based[4] means not eating any foods that have animals or animal byproducts in them. Being a vegan goes into a whole new world of restrictions due to cross-contamination during the food preparation process, as well as choosing clothes, brands to support, animal testing, and more. I enjoy the freedom of not having to worry about what or how my food is prepared. Additionally, grilling is one of my favorite hobbies, so the vegan lifestyle wouldn't be great for me. My choice not to be vegan, however, doesn't mean that I am a detractor of vegans or an advocate for the mistreatment of animals.

Herein lies the struggle. Many vegans can be emotional and openly opinionated about their beliefs. They have a loyalty to their convictions that means they cannot go to just any restaurant or purchase any food they want without reading the ingredient list, which is an action many of us have become accustomed to not having to do. Vegans want to be listened to and heard to get people to understand their cause, and who can blame them when they put forth so much effort into sticking to their beliefs? In doing so, many have become quite good at expressing their opinions and emotions on the matter, since many non-vegans will question their restricted diet.

The responses to questioning vegans can vary. On both sides, we can hear jokes and ridicule meant to hurt others. This is where we can practice our listening skills and respect one another's choices. There is a way to positively influence people to understand your side without being negative or bringing them down. This brings us back to values, justification, the high road, accountability, and being humble. We can all grow to be better listeners and accept that not everyone will follow the same path as us.

---

4. For the sake of this argument, I will not continue to differentiate between those who eat plant-based diets and those who are vegan. To keep the discussion simpler, I will only use the word "vegan."

Listening is not the same as agreeing. Listening is just the first step to getting along, which will lead to us having a better understanding of one another. By listening to what people say through their words and actions, we can begin to understand the true context by which people are trying to influence.

Having a vegan daughter has taught me that vegans just want people to understand their choice. Of course, they wish that those of us who are not vegan would align with them and become vegans too. But who doesn't want that when they stand for something they believe in? My family member's choice to be vegan rarely affects me. In fact, it gives me a listening and learning opportunity, which is the crux of my lesson here. I've had the opportunity to watch as Mary influences my son, Henry, in becoming pescatarian. In fact, he is even more emotional than his sister about factory farming and the benefits of organic living.

There is so much to be learned from others, but only if we take the time to listen and understand their perspective. Listening is how we expand ourselves and our positive influence. By engaging others in "proactive listening," we can search for context and clarity, giving us a more open line of communication with the other person. Proactive listening is a step above productive listening: It's when we actively listen to learn (productive listening) but with a mindset that we need to gather more information to build deeper context. Proactive listening generally requires the listener to ask more questions based on what has been communicated to them already. Proactive listening can build a deeper human connection, allowing for more open dialogue.

Therefore, by interacting with others proactively, instead of reactively, we will become fairer and more objective individuals in all aspects of life. Listening allows us to be more pragmatic. As we practice listening, we are changing our internal data-collection habits; we can learn to become more pragmatic toward the myriad of issues we face. We can always stand to gain more positive influence by becoming more fair, objective, and pragmatic.

Key Takeaways: Listening

- Listening is an art that requires you to hear what the other person is saying while also understanding your reactions, emotions, and opinions of what you are hearing. Listening to yourself can help you understand your mind.
- Listening is not the same as agreeing. Listening is just the first step to getting along, which will lead to you having a better understanding of others.
- Productive listening is when you acknowledge, even just to yourself, whether or not the person you are speaking with is also listening. Proactive listening is when you combine productive listening (actively listening) with the desire to gather more information to build deeper context.
- One of the best ways to engage in listening is by asking thoughtful, open-ended questions, as this shows that you are trying to gather more context.

Fair and Objective

To understand our influence, we must understand our bias, which we'll discuss a bit more in Chapter 6. Each of us has bias toward different things based on our perception of the world and our life circumstances. If we attempt to understand our bias—and I say "attempt" because we are only human—then we can move towards becoming more objective.

Understanding ourselves and where we come from will allow us to identify what our opinions are and where *they* come from. Opinions are typically rooted in some bias based on our values. When we understand our opinions and the bias that roots them, we are better prepared for discussions with those who have opposing opinions. We can enter these discussions with open ears and minds. Even if we don't change our opinion, we can listen and respect that someone else has an opinion different than ours. This is what moves us towards being fair. One of the challenges of this section is to define what is "fair" due to its subjectivity.

Fairness is generally accepted as adhering to laws, policies, or procedures, but even these areas were created by humans with opinions and motivations, thereby providing them with a certain amount of bias. This is important for us to understand because part of the responsibility of our influence is to allow for objective discussions about things that we already believe to be fair. Nothing in life is fair or objective. There will always be some type of disparity amongst humans. However, how we approach this disparity is our responsibility. Allowing ourselves to be open to others' views of the world allows us to further our knowledge and positive influence, and pushes us towards being fairer and more objective, not just for our teams but also in life.

Please note that being fair isn't about being on the "correct" side of issues because, again, we may all feel that we are "correct." Being fair is about being open to new information and having respect for a fellow human's right to free speech. It is absurd to think that we will all have the same opinions on issues, but it *is* reasonable to have a discussion based on opinions. Conversing with those with opposing views gives us an opportunity to learn about the perspective of someone else; it doesn't mean we have to change our minds. Being fair means setting aside personal emotions and qualms while maintaining integrity in our values.

By understanding our limits and, therefore, the limits that laws, policies, and procedures have, we can move forward with constructing what may be fair. Then, we can communicate more effectively our aversion towards the laws, policies, and procedures we do not agree with. We can find faults in ourselves, or in the system, and choose whether to exploit those faults objectively or not. There will absolutely be times when it will be hard to remain objective simply due to ignorance—we don't know what we don't know.

If you find yourself in a situation where you find it hard to remain objective—typically in situations that contradict your values or what you believe in—try to notice that you are having a hard time remaining objective. Once you train your mind to take notice of those moments, it will get easier. Some of the best ways to become objective are to learn what you can on the subject from all sides, listen and ask follow-up questions, accept when you may be wrong, and perhaps change your views. This is immensely difficult when you battle confirmation bias, but to be a positive leader, you owe it to yourself and your teams to do your best to open your mind up to other possibilities.

There have been a few times when I have put my foot in my mouth or acted on something prior to understanding the limits. For example, I have placed restrictions on my team out of ego by not allowing them to perform certain tasks or engage in conversations out of my need to micromanage the project. This act is contradictory to what we stand for at IA, where we intend to bring together the best minds to work on a problem as a team. Mine is not always the best mind. I can be unfair to my team by not allowing them to grow and engage in the problem. In these cases, I'm not being objective about my lack of understanding, or my ego gets in the way of my ability to be fair.

If I had stepped back and realized I did not need to micromanage, I would have been able to delegate to my team. As a leader, you must contemplate what is fair for the team. In doing so, you must be mindful not to discriminate, as any kind of discrimination is unfair. Rather, you must remain objective, which may force you to remove yourself from the situation and think from another's perspective. If you find this difficult, be honest. Being honest with your team about your shortcomings will allow you to all come together in support.

Sometimes our emotions get in the way of us being fair, especially if we don't have a basis for understanding what is fair. In those instances, our emotions can often fill in the gaps. When we feel our emotions kicking in, we must push to be the most fair and objective we can be. By allowing our emotions to take over what we intend to be a fair and objective conversation, we immediately challenge the notion of fair and objective responsibility. This doesn't mean that we need to eliminate our emotion. Instead, those of us who are emotionally mature can use our emotion to influence others through concise and objective communication. The goal should be to influence those in a positive way and allow for people to challenge us along the way if they disagree.

Today, society dictates the definition of fairness through laws. Some believe that those laws are fair, while others believe they are unfair. This subjectivity makes the topic hard to navigate as each of our definitions of fair will vary. However, if you are to be a positive, influential leader, you need to understand on a deeper level how you apply being fair. Fairness is dictated by individuals based on the environment they are presently living in, and fairness should be understood by this context.

The reality is that fairness is amazingly difficult for leaders because there are so many other nuances that tear at our emotions, our faith, and even our very existence as humans. We are masters at taking on a cause for others and doing extraordinary things for them—until that cause has a negative effect on us personally. Then, our position can drive us from a generally pragmatic position of support into a frenzy of emotions that can tip us into imbalance.

Our access to immediate notifications and news has made it harder for some to separate their emotions from what they believe is fair. The speed at which information is shared is fueling the speed at which emotions get triggered, which can cause a groundswell that creates a tipping point for people with influence to make decisions that are not well thought out or understood. The context is lost, and the result is an environment that becomes unfair or even untenable. Understanding this about people, and likely about ourselves, is the best way to try to tip the scales back to fairness. If we can come to terms with the fact that our emotions are being played by people who wish to influence us unfairly, we can slow down the spread of information that is creating the negative environment.

Key Takeaways: Fair and Objective

- Being fair means respecting everyone's right to free speech, while being objective means understanding that there are differing views in the world without sacrificing your point of view.
- You can move toward being fair by first understanding your values and opinions and exploring if you have any bias rooted in them. When you understand yourself, you can communicate with others who may not see the world from the same perspective in an objective way. You don't have to change your opinions or values to be fair and objective.
- If you allow your emotions to take over, you may compromise your ability to be fair and objective. This doesn't mean you need to abandon emotion; it means you should try to develop more emotional intelligence so you can use your emotions to positively influence others.

Understand the Responsibility Reflection

The weight of our responsibility to have a positive influence may seem daunting, but it doesn't have to be. By first *recognizing* that we each have a powerful influence, we will begin to understand our responsibility. However, understanding the responsibility of our influence also comes with recognizing that we will fail, and we will make mistakes. None of us are perfect, so we must have empathy for ourselves and others during those times. When we understand and hold responsibility for our influence, we can step more fully into being positive leaders who make a difference.

CHAPTER 3

PITFALLS

> **"I must try to live in society and yet remain untouched by its pitfalls."**
> **—Mahatma Gandhi**

Each time I look at this chapter, I struggle with the name: *Pitfalls*. When I think of a pitfall, I think of those covered traps in cartoons or movies that people fall into, sometimes laden with spikes or other nasty surprises along the bottom, while others are just pits to trap that person until they are rescued or find a way out. In the movies, as in real life, people will fall into the pit repeatedly, never quite learning the lessons needed to get around or out of the pit.

In terms of my definition for this chapter, pitfalls are created by the consequences of our actions; they may or may not be purposeful, meaning we can encounter intended or unintended pitfalls. I generally believe that we *unintentionally* create most of our pitfalls by not properly analyzing our thoughts, words, and actions. Therefore, they can result from inexperience, not preparing for situations, self-sabotage, and more. And when we don't fully grasp the responsibility of our influence, there are pitfalls that come with that, too. The same goes for when we aren't honest or humble, or when we allow our ego to run our life. Oftentimes, when we fail to properly analyze a situation or ourselves, unintended consequences can turn into pitfalls that prove to be detrimental to our present and future wellbeing.

To give you an example, I would like to look at weight loss and dieting. There are several variables that go into weight loss, one of them being the food you put into your body. The boom in commercial weight-loss programs/fads has developed a wide range of weight-loss programs for people of all shapes and sizes. For me, the biggest pitfall on my weight-loss journey, in terms of sticking to a program, has been not consistently losing weight. For example, I have tried the Atkins diet. It was amazing when I followed it correctly. I rapidly dropped weight, but then I would plateau. I didn't understand this weight plateau, which happened in several other programs I tried as well. I believe that this weight plateau was a pitfall, and I kept falling into it program after program.

I believe this weight plateau was a pitfall for me because I didn't *understand* it was a pitfall. From program to program, I didn't learn the meaning behind the weight plateau and continued to fall into the same trap. When I began doing some digging, I found that one of the common problems for those trying to lose weight is the dreaded weight-loss plateau. Like many others, during my weight-loss journey, I was only focused on a number (how many pounds I shed that week) rather than measuring how I felt physically and mentally. By defining my success based on one number, I had set myself up for the plateau pitfall. Only by researching, gaining more insight into this phenomenon, and setting other ways to measure my goal was I able to begin avoiding the pitfall.

If you want to look for the pitfalls in your life—because, I assure you, you have many—you need to first accept that you have some. Sometimes, they are hard to spot. But if you can take time to reflect on the things in your life that you struggle with (e.g., making decisions, communicating openly, etc.), then you can identify some of the common denominators to your pitfalls. Think about any consequences you have had or accountability you may have experienced. The consistency between the consequences and accountability may surprise you and point right to your most prevalent pitfalls.

As a leader, there are several pitfalls that you'll need to be on the lookout for, not just for yourself but for your team as well. Pitfalls can undeniably ruin relationships, challenge work culture, and destroy companies or even countries. Pitfalls can harm people physically, emotionally, and psychologically. Our goal is to help you understand pitfalls, even unanticipated or unknown ones, so you can be more conscious and mindful about avoiding them. Even great leaders and influencers fall prey to pitfalls.

For example, your inability to grasp your emotional responses to issues, or your loss of composure, can create pitfalls, like pushing people out of your life without meaning to. If the people around you disengage by shying away, avoiding, or flat-out removing you from their lives, you are missing out on the opportunity and advantage that such interactions may have had. You can understand those missed opportunities as metaphors for falling into the pit and being held captive by emotional outbursts that can alienate and destroy your relationships. If this happens often, you may ask yourself why people continue to disengage with you or why they avoid you. What pitfall are you causing for yourself? An inability to control reactions or internal feelings can result in others being affected or damaged by your influence.

So, in these cases, why do people create pitfalls? Pitfalls are typically a defense mechanism because people believe they are protecting something. For example, values can be a pitfall, or at least can create unintended consequences. Let's take religious or political values, for instance. These values can become a pitfall depending on the environments you are in, the company you keep, and how you adhere to them. You can lose friends or loved ones depending on the values you align with, or you may become a hypocrite, stating you believe one thing but behaving in another way altogether.

One of the most prevalent causes of pitfalls, which has been mentioned several times in this series, is ego. We discuss ego repetitively because, quite often, individuals fuel their ego based on the amount of responsibility they have; they create pitfalls in support of that ego. For example, when a boss treats people as if they are below them and tries to inspire them with grandiose statements or affluent purchases, they create an environment where people feel devalued and used. The pitfall is that these unappreciated people will eventually leave, along with their particular skills and talents.

Pitfalls can also occur when we take people or situations for granted. When we expect that a person will react a certain way or that something will have a specific outcome, we create potential pitfalls that set us up for failure. For example, say every Monday morning, you rely on a report from a team member to complete your work. However, one Monday, that team member is out for an emergency. What happens if they are the only one who knows how to run the report? Taking for granted that they will always be there Monday morning and not knowing how to run the report if they aren't there sets you up to fail in your own tasks. Thus, you've created the pitfall of taking someone for granted, which is a lot like making an assumption. When we assume something is going to happen a certain way because it has happened that way in the past, we take that thing for granted. Or we set ourselves up for disappointment when that event fails to deliver what, in our minds, was promised.

Another pitfall happens when we are disingenuous—when we say something that we don't mean or believe to be true. We may feel that there are no consequences for failing to follow through on our promises with action or for not behaving in a way that aligns with what we claim to believe, but there are. Being disingenuous means our ego may be interfering with our ability to influence positively. Disingenuous people may not be found out immediately, but, in time, people will notice. How? By being inconsistent or leading with a "Do as I say, not as I do" attitude. When that pitfall comes, those who are disingenuous will reap the consequences, which usually entail loss of friendship, family, or job.

On the bright side, you can anticipate pitfalls once you realize they are there. Because life's pitfalls can be camouflaged by your actions, personalities, and idiosyncrasics, my hope is to help you realize not only how certain pitfalls influence you, but how to anticipate and avoid them. However, if you find yourself stuck in a pit, don't assume you will never find a way out. There is always a way, and we are here to lend you a hand.

Assumptions

Never *ass-u-me,* because you will make an *ass* out of *you* and *me.* I always thought that was such a snarky play on words, but it's also true. Assuming is one of our most prolific pitfalls. I am also guilty of making assumptions, even though it is one of the most common lessons I teach people every day. It's hard to kick the habit of assuming, even when you're working hard to do so. But in order to have a positive influence on your teams, you must try to prevent yourself from acting upon your assumptions. Though there are several types of assumptions, too many to lay out in this book, we will cover a few.

All assumptions are a guess, often based on facts or experience, but nevertheless, still a guess. Taking it a step further, a blind assumption is something we take for granted, some kind of predicted occurrence. For example, there are financial assumptions that are modeled after factual data, like the economy or the stock market. While these things have a low margin for error, they aren't always correct. Take predicting the weather, for example. How many times have you looked at your weather app, assumed it was correct, only to come to the day you had planned something and it's raining? Predictions, even if they are made scientifically, are still assumptions waiting to happen. Assumptions are just guesses, even if they are *educated* guesses.

I believe that most of our personal assumptions—ones that aren't determined by a formula—are generally bred out of impatience or laziness; we don't want to slow down or take the time to understand what or whom we are assuming about. By not slowing down and trying to understand the *what* or *whom*, if we know all we need to, we risk depriving ourselves of information and growth that could have enhanced our influence. We miss out on the opportunity to learn.

Perception is another tool we use to create assumptions. Our perceptions of the world, which sometimes boil down to our *assumptions* of the world, can make us forget about the opportunities and advantages possible when we push our boundaries. However, it can also make us forget about the risks that come from assuming. By slowing down, we can get ahead of ourselves and proactively tackle our assumptions about the world. We can challenge our perceptions and beliefs.

For example, say you envy someone in your industry for having a better car, house, or family. They live a lavish lifestyle, yet they are in the same industry as you. You think "I could do that" without considering the other possibilities about that person's lifestyle. They may have a partner who has a high-paying job, or they may come from "old money." You need to be able to expand your mind to other possibilities so you can question your perceptions of the world and let go of your assumptions. You must also be honest about your assumptions and the emotions attached to them. Remain objective and consider the potential influence those things can have on you.

Lastly, you can make assumptions about ideas. I chose to discuss this last because it can have a dramatic effect on how you influence others. All your ideas deserve to be observed, understood, and challenged so that you can have a positive influence—from small, seemingly unimportant ideas, like what topping to put on your toast in the morning, to more influential ideas, like making dramatic changes to your life, home, or business. The assumptions you create based on your ideas can have a dramatic impact on your influence as leaders.

The Downfall of Delegation

I personally make a lot of assumptions that create pitfalls for me. I justify this pitfall because it is attached to another leadership trait I have: Delegation. I tend to delegate to a fault, which is where my assumptions run rampant. Therefore, delegation can be a pitfall when it's not used properly. The best story I have to explain how my assumptions turned my trait of delegating into a pitfall is when we moved IA from Oregon to Illinois in 2013.

We had just completed the sale of YourBizDr.com, and our largest investment asset outside of IA was in Illinois. As with our other offices, our Illinois office was to be embedded into the offices of other companies we owned and with whom we provide advisory services. We do this so we can work more closely with our clients and adjacent team members to help each other further in our areas of influence.

Following this move, I changed our hiring process—I stopped participating in it. I delegated the hiring process to others in our organization. We had a successful hiring process for years, so by delegating, I assumed that my team would follow this same process. This included having an in-depth understanding of our new or potential hire's strengths, weaknesses, and abilities. However, I didn't clearly explain the purpose for our hiring, what we would be using the new hire for, and how that new hire would be expected to interact with the team and our clients.

To put it nicely, delegating the hiring process to my team proved to be a disaster, and not because of anything my team did incorrectly. No, quite the contrary. The team performed amazingly well, considering the fact they were not trained to perform hiring services. The disaster came from my assumption that they would know what I already knew. They asked the standard questions outlined in the policy, but they did not know how to ask further questions to paint a full picture of that individual or how to prepare them for the environment they were being hired for. My team had little to no understanding of my full intentions and reasons for hiring a new person, yet I assumed they could complete this task. Therefore, after delegating the hiring process to my team, we hired Lloyd (a fake name).

On the surface, Lloyd seemed like the perfect candidate to become a new team member and help us with our clients. However, after roughly 18 to 24 months of working with Lloyd, we were struggling to manage client projects. These failures were isolated to Lloyd's projects, but as I have mentioned several times, I delegate to a fault. While I realized the common denominator to these issues was, in fact, Lloyd, I took responsibility for those mistakes, too, as I had delegated those tasks to Lloyd as his leader. I owned the projects just as much as he did. I was in full delegation mode as we were extremely busy, and I felt that as long as we could mitigate our mistakes and keep learning as a team, we would continue to grow Individually.

After working to keep up with struggling projects, I decided we should hire another associate to join our team. However, the newest associate (let's call him Harry) was hired using the same process as when we hired Lloyd, except this time, Lloyd was part of the hiring process. Now, we had Lloyd and Harry working for our team, and I hoped they would help us manage our clients and scale our business in the Chicago area. Unfortunately, as I am sure you have guessed, hiring Harry with the same procedure (which wasn't our typical procedure) as we used to hire Lloyd was a huge mistake. Our team saw the same issues with Harry as we did with Lloyd. Their failures were similar: unhappy clients, unhappy team members, poor results, and a negative shift in company culture.

Despite the negativity Lloyd and Harry brought with them due to their egos and generally negative attitudes, the team continued to strive for a positive team culture. The team openly discussed the challenges they had with Lloyd and Harry, but we were getting negative comments from clients about their performance as well. My first inclination was to make our clients happy and get them back on track for success. I don't look for who to blame first, as this doesn't get the team or the client anywhere. As I became more educated on the issues that Lloyd and Harry were causing, my focus was on the resolution and not the people who caused it. Eventually, the issues with Lloyd and Harry wore on my team, and it became progressively more difficult to stay positive. They opened up about how it was affecting them, and soon enough, they wanted me to act against Lloyd and Harry. Every other conversation seemed to be about their failures and the effects of those failures, and the team became very vocal about their inability to work with and trust either Lloyd or Harry.

Still, Lloyd and Harry were not terminated immediately. I decided to compartmentalize their authority over projects to tasks that they *needed* to be involved in and could positively contribute to. Additionally, I encouraged them to participate in the resolution of the issues we were facing with our clients, under my direct authority; it was my version of accountability without overtly declaring it "accountability." I had not yet researched the underlying accusations brought by my team that caused these issues in the first place, choosing instead to focus on the specific issues created. It wasn't that I didn't believe my team, but I was focused on alleviating the client issues first.

Once the client-facing issues were resolved, I went back to determine who or what had caused them. As you know, the issues were a direct result of poor oversight and bad leadership from Lloyd,

Harry, and me. However, the ultimate mistake lies with me because I chose to delegate the hiring process to my team and assumed they would know exactly how to carry out the same approach I had. This failure resulted in our team hiring individuals who were not capable of performing the work we needed. Then, I failed to integrate Lloyd and Harry into our IA culture and provide the tools and leadership necessary for success. In creating this environment, I failed the company, our team, and our clients by shortcutting my own standards and ignoring my team.

Assumptions can become a pitfall for anyone. I knew better than to assume that standard hiring policies could prepare someone for the complexities of the human mind. Even knowing this now, I still delegate to a fault occasionally and assume that the person I am delegating tasks and responsibilities to will be able to handle what I am relying on them for. Luckily, after our abysmal five-year hiring fiasco, I am now back to a team that was properly hired and understands my propensity to delegate. We, as a team, do not make assumptions about each other; we communicate openly and have an understanding for each other's faults and pitfalls.

Sweating the Small Stuff

We all suffer from assumptions that can influence our lives, whether at work, home, with friends, or even alone; we must actively try to manage our assumptions, which requires us to understand what impacts our assumptions. Any assumptions we make that involve other people in our lives—when we assume someone will act a certain way or perform a specific action—have the potential to create conflict. Assumptions about human behavior can be dangerous because we each have a way of doing things for reasons only we may understand.

By assuming that an idea is beneficial for us or those we influence, and choosing to move forward on that assumption, we are taking a chance based on our assumption that our idea is good. Many people make decisions based on assumptions. Unfortunately, many small businesses start based on assumptions. In fact, they should call the dream of owning a small business in America an assumption. While not all small business ideas fail, many do.

The majority of small businesses are based on ideas grounded in wishful thinking, which is likely why the majority of those new small businesses fail. Eighty percent of small businesses fail quickly because the owner allows assumption to be the primary decision-maker. For example, one of the most common assumptions I see businesses make (which I touched on briefly earlier) is the assumption that just because another company did something, it means they can do the same thing. Making assumptions based on another's performance is very dangerous, primarily because our perceptions and context are skewed.

Allow me to give you two more examples to expand on this idea, one successful and one not. The first is in the medical field, and it was *not* successful. One of our clients came to us to develop a business plan with the intention of raising funds for the business. Early in the process, we stressed that while they felt very positive about their business idea (as we did), they were going to need to lay the foundation of funding through personal contacts. Their response was, "No problem, we know hundreds of people who are excited about our idea."

The business plan was very complex; the business itself, in the medical field, required a ton of research. The totality of the project was such that we were engaging with state and local officials, as well as real estate agents, architects, equipment suppliers, and more. The market for this business was very robust, and there was a definite need for what this client was attempting to create. When the first draft of our business plan was finished, we wanted to introduce it to the hundreds of contacts our clients had mentioned at the beginning. Having friendly people take a first peek would have given us the opportunity to get objective feedback and make refinements before we took it to an open market.

Unfortunately, not a single person from the contacts our client provided us invested a dime. In fact, not even the client invested a dime. Yet, they assumed that if we took it to our professional contacts, just the fact that our firm backed it would give it enough credibility to get funded. Despite our repeated admonishments, they continued to assume that all it would take is a credible company to present the "plan" and people would just line up and jump on board. Even after explaining that they needed to become credible themselves by either investing or giving up control, they continued to assume that we could get them funded because it was a great idea. The devil is in the details, which is why assumptions fail; assumptions skip the details and give the devil a foothold to screw up a great idea.

This leads me to the second example where a client made an assumption; thankfully, we were able to slow down the process and turn their early assumption into a later success. In this case, our client had patents. Patents sound like a very cool thing, but they can also be very lucrative. When we began working with this client, they had filed patents and some had been awarded. Our client was generating revenue, but the losses were high—over one million dollars in the first five years.

When we were retained to help, I noticed that their marketing effort was largely based on the assumption that people would buy the product due to its patent. The owner of the company found his value in being an inventor, so all his efforts went into inventing things that he assumed would be marketable once he was done. Once we slowed the company down and understood what the products were designed to do, we were able to work with the company to begin selling their products. Instead of assuming that people would buy the product because it was patented, we tied the value of the product to the problems it solved.

The assumptions we have about our own ideas are one of the most dangerous pitfalls we can fall into. Because it's our idea, we think it's great; we assume that other people will think it's great, too.

We assume that if we put up a website, people will just happen upon it and buy our products or services. We assume that because our friends and family encourage us, we don't need to do the groundwork or perform the due diligence necessary to understand what is truly needed to fulfill our brilliant idea. A business idea needs to be desirable (do people want it?), feasible (can it be built/executed?), and viable (can it make money?).

This doesn't mean we have to stop having ideas or dreaming big; it just means that we need to stop assuming that our ideas are always going to be the best ones. People want to own their ideas as their own "thing" due to ego, but ego is the foundation of assumption. In fact, our ideas come from a culmination of all we have learned from the individuals who have influenced us throughout our lives. When you have a seemingly good idea you want to act upon, slow down and allow for a little due diligence to reinforce (or challenge) that you have a good idea. It may even prove to give you more information to change and clarify your idea so that it is more successful.

If we fail to perform due diligence and our assumptions fail, it can be incredibly damaging. We are often surprised when our ideas fail, especially when we assumed that they would succeed. This surprise comes from our ego; our ego created our initial assumption, and we didn't anticipate anything but self-fulfilling positive feelings coming from our idea. The surprise can lead to justification for why it failed, instead of performing due diligence to find out why it failed. This justification will influence us not to see or understand the true failure, which will cycle us back into making more assumptions. When we tackle assumptions from the root, we can get our ideas back on the right track. The success of slowing down and not assuming will ultimately feed our egos in more positive ways. If we know something is a sure thing after we've done our due diligence, then it is no longer an assumption. If that "sure thing" does not come to fruition, then we need to slow down and backtrack to our assumptions in order to gain an understanding of where we went wrong in labeling it a sure thing.

Slowing down your mind enough to get out of the habit of assuming may require a trigger—something to signal you're making an assumption. It could be a word, outsourced accountability, or even just being more open-minded. If you find yourself not being able to answer questions you or someone else has about your decisions, you have made an assumption. Make sure everyone is on the same page and has thought through the scenario to the best of everyone's capabilities. Asking questions and focusing your attention is a great byproduct of slowing down. This approach can help you restart your project or avoid having the same issues in the future with a new project.

Working to Overcome Assumptions

One of the best reasons to never assume is that it is better to be surprised than disappointed. If we assume that someone will do something for us, but they don't, that often leads to disappointment and conflict. If we enter with a mindset where we don't assume that the people around us will behave and perform in a certain way, we can elevate our influence to a more positive level. We set ourselves up to be surprised (positive) rather than creating a pitfall for ourselves to be disappointed (negative).

In addition to making assumptions about the people in our lives, we can make assumptions about places and things. For example, we may assume that because we get great service, coffee, and scones at our local Starbucks, we will receive the same at all Starbucks locations. (We assume this because of the policies and procedures Starbucks has in place for all their franchises, as we discussed earlier in this book.) This assumption can set us up for disappointment and perhaps even anger if we are let down. However—and I have experienced this first-hand with several chain restaurants around the globe—just because one location is great doesn't mean that all locations are great. Other common assumptions also often fall into this thought process: If we have consistently experienced something with a person or place, we accept that experience as fact, assuming that our experience will be the same every time. Unfortunately, life rarely works out that way.

We can take small and big things in our lives for granted and assume that they will always be up to par with how we remember them. One example of this is smoke detectors. I am not sure how many of us actually check to make sure our smoke detectors are working, but I know at least some of us just assume that they will. Then we are reminded of them at 2:00 a.m. when the "low battery" beeping starts and wakes the entire household. Of course, this is a simple example, but there are many things in our lives that we make assumptions about that can affect us emotionally and physically.

One of the best ways to avoid making assumptions is to slow down and remember the small details. Don't assume that your flash-light or smoke or carbon monoxide detectors are working. Don't assume that your car's spare is good; have it checked when you service your vehicle. Don't wait until there is something you rely on in rare situations to learn that it is not operating correctly—be proactive instead of assuming.

We can also fall prey to the assumption that an event will be good or bad, which can rob us of an opportunity. There have been countless times that René and I have attended an event "out of obligation," meaning we really didn't want to go because we assumed we would not enjoy it, and it turned out that we had a remarkable time. It usually turns out that we meet cool people and learn new things that we wouldn't have had we chosen not to go due to our assumptions.

Most assumptions can be resolved through communication, by asking questions and listening. This means we must rely on ourselves and others to have honest communication. We can eliminate some of the negative aspects of assuming by being consistent in our actions and recognizing our tendencies to assume as a function of our laziness. We can counter this tendency by asking one more question, making one more comment, or giving the issue or idea one more moment.

The goal of reducing our assumptions—because, let's face it, it would be difficult to fully eliminate our tendency to assume—is to create an environment where we have more control over our actions and influence. When we have achieved that environment, it's important not to take our teams for granted. Just because we may expect our actions and influence to remain consistent doesn't make it fair for us to assume that others will also remain consistent in their actions and influence.

Key Takeaways: Assumptions

- All assumptions are a guess, often based on fact or experience (perception), but they are your way of filling in context when you don't understand or don't take the time to slow down and ask questions.
- Managing your assumptions will require you to understand what influences your decisions to create those assumptions. Is it a need to be correct? A fear of asking questions to gain more context?
- Don't make assumptions when it comes to moving forward with an idea. Not performing the proper due diligence can cause failure down the road. Your business idea needs to be desirable, feasible, and viable.

Taking (I)individuals for Granted

We all get used to certain situations in our lives. Circumstances become comfortable, people do things for us habitually, and then, before we know it, we are taking people or situations for granted. Taking a person for granted can work in one of two ways. First, we can expect good things to come from them. Second, we can expect bad things to come from them. This is something that correlates with our assumptions because when we take people for granted, we are assuming that they will continue doing exactly what we expect them to do.

We also create *environments* where we take things or people for granted. With technology and the overwhelming inclination to streamline everything, we create systems and situations that are intended to make our lives simpler by setting expectations. Once those expectations are met, we begin to expect the same results every time. One of the most common places where we create these expectations—and sometimes rightly so—is at work, where policies and procedures can lay the foundation for us to take things or people for granted.

In our work environments, when we follow policies and procedures, we tend to expect that others will do the same. We, therefore, take for granted that others will approach tasks and problems in the way that the policies and procedures lay out. When we expect others to follow policies and procedures, we can take those people for granted and lose our ability to be grateful for their actions—chalking it up to "it's their job." Losing the ability to be grateful means losing the ability to be a positive and influential leader.

I work in various offices around the country. There is a large base of people who support the various companies that I influence daily when carrying out my responsibilities. I am often asked how I manage to keep the various clients and companies organized, all while writing a book series, developing a podcast, and engaging in a variety of speaking arrangements. As I previously mentioned, I delegate often, sometimes to a fault. However, I believe that the people I'm delegating tasks to are capable, and I know that without them, I could never do it all. There is no way I would be able to effectively lead without eliminating the act of taking people for granted.

Does this mean that I don't take people for granted? Well, no, I'm only human. Like everyone else, I fall into that terrible place where I expect people to do things and assume certain actions will transpire. I believe I have every right to expect that these are going to happen, day in and day out; what I don't have is the right to take people for granted. I strive to identify and acknowledge that part of what they do is the reason I am successful and have my position.

One of the greatest lessons I have learned is that no one is a leader alone. Being a leader is about having a positive influence on people in all areas of your life. The influence you have as a leader comes with tremendous responsibility. You are regularly plowing a way for your team to have more influence, all while keeping yourself focused and positive. This way, you can empower your team to feel good about what they contribute to the goals of the company.

Leaders who come in, bark commands, set unrealistic expectations, or ignore their surroundings aren't really utilizing their leadership and influence in a positive way. These actions show that these leaders are taking their team for granted, which is where many foundational issues are found: Companies are picked apart and lose the advantages rooted in their teams and themselves.

A common practice we see in small businesses that reflects the above lack of leadership is when business owners and managers equate doing "nice things" for their employees with being a good manager. One of our clients was struggling with high turnover; they seemed to be losing people between 12 and 18 months after hiring. Each time they lost someone, that individual was very negative about the experience they had working for our client. It was hard to put into context at first because the client would paint the picture of each lost employee's tenure at the company as ideal. However, this is what our client thought was ideal: They loaned employees money when asked, offered time off when asked, and provided other material things when asked. Meaning they thought they could buy their employees' loyalty in small bits over time.

We also learned that the organization was highly dysfunctional. For one thing, the work schedules were sporadic. The consistency of hours was non-existent, meaning someone would work 25 hours one week and 45 the next. On top of that, the work itself was difficult. The company had a lot of equipment issues and lost clients often, although they replaced them often, too. So, they had high employee and customer turnover—a recipe for disaster. Moreover, management and ownership were not consistently involved in supporting the work of their team. Ultimately, it was a hostile work environment for the employees.

Our client was surprised whenever anyone would quit. Their reaction to someone quitting was often an overreaction. The first time I experienced this with them, I asked why they thought the person had a negative experience. Their reply was, "I don't know; I loaned them money and gave them what they were asking. I treated them great." That is when I had to explain that our client was taking their employees for granted. They were creating a hostile work environment for their employees and trying to justify it by performing small, superficial favors that were often too little, too late. They took their employees for granted because they thought they could buy loyalty and credibility in the short term.

One of the byproducts of taking someone or something for granted is that we become susceptible to being disingenuous. When we first ask someone to do something for us, those of us with manners will use the words "please" and "thank you." As we work with and spend more time with people, we get used to the things they do for us. Over time, we may stop using "please" and "thank you," and at this time, we begin taking those people's actions for granted.

Once we begin to take people for granted, our pleasantries and thankful attitude may disintegrate. By being disingenuous, we hurt ourselves more than we hurt the person doing something for us. Therefore, when we take someone for granted, it becomes a pitfall to being a good influence on our teams. Positive influence means we respect people, remember the things they do for us, recognize those efforts, and act accordingly. By taking others' actions for granted, we don't respect ourselves or them.

Another reason we may fall prey to the pitfall of taking people or situations for granted is that we don't demonstrate transparency, meaning we lack open and honest communication. For example, we may have a team member who performs a task that seems simple. However, if we don't ask our team member what that task is like for them, or inquire more into the task itself, we may take our team member for granted, thinking their task is simple. This assumption can sometimes come with negative feelings, such as envy for not being responsible for such a seemingly simple task. This is when we may begin to take that team member and task for granted because we lack the transparency to learn all that the task entails for our team member. When we lack details, we lack transparency; this can create a pitfall.

By choosing to be transparent with your team, either by asking questions or offering information willingly, you can set realistic expectations supported by accountability. On one side, if you don't communicate and remain transparent with your team, you may be the one who is taken for granted, as others don't realize the influence of your role. On the other side, if you don't ask your team questions to gain a better understanding of the role of their influence, you may take them for granted. Start conversations early and be mindful to always check up afterward. Don't fall into the trap of assuming you can have one conversation and be done. Transparency requires continuous effort.

When you promote continuous, open communication, you create a team culture of not taking each other for granted. When your team doesn't have the information they need, they remain ignorant on that subject. Meaning you can't blame them for taking you for granted due to their ignorance because you can't blame others for what they don't know. Ignorance can lead to others taking you for granted, bringing us back to the importance of transparency. Additionally, ignorance plays a key role in taking others for granted. Now, one of the most common misconceptions is that if you call someone ignorant, then you are calling them stupid. That is not the case. Ignorance is defined as lacking awareness, knowledge, or education on a particular topic; it does not mean that a person is stupid.

Ignorance is born out of many things. In controllable situations, ignorance becomes a pitfall to taking others for granted. There are times when being ignorant may work in your favor, meaning that if you don't know something, someone else who is more equipped might take care of that something for you. If this is done enough, however, then it will become an expectation, and you run the risk of taking that something or someone for granted.

This can become an issue because, regardless of whether it is conscious or subconscious, you come to expect that "something" to be done for you when you are capable of learning the task yourself. For example, at our IA office, we have a large cubicle area where four team members sit outside my office. My door faces Brenda who is, for all intents and purposes, the most important person in my life when I am working in the office. She helps me more than anyone else as far as my day-to-day responsibilities go. Brenda is my keeper of information, information that is readily available to our whole team through the cloud.

Yet, nearly on a daily basis, I will yell out to her, "What is the password for XYZ company?" and, thankfully, Brenda will find it for me. Sometimes, I'll ask her to send me a certain document we have, and, shortly after, I'll hear that email *bing*. There have been times I have sat and waited patiently, and I will get no *bing*. I'll peek around my office door and notice that Brenda is not there. It's times like these that I think I could (and should) learn how to use our cloud-based system properly.

Learning how to perform tasks that our team has mastered can make us more beneficial to our team. It increases our positive influence as we move forward because we will be available when one of our team members needs us. When we don't take the time to learn how to do what our team members can do, we may wind up taking them for granted. This isn't to say that we must know how to do everything, because each of us brings something different to the team for a reason. It just means that the whole team can all learn small things whenever possible.

Taking people and situations for granted will ultimately catch up to the person doing it. Each time we take someone or something for granted, we create a pitfall for ourselves and diminish our positive influence. One of the leading contributors of making people feel taken for granted is when we over-delegate. Delegation is an important trait in positive leadership, but it can also be a pitfall that leads us right back to taking people for granted.

Key Takeaways: Taking (I)individuals for Granted

- You may take someone for granted by expecting them to do good (or bad) things, coupled with your assumptions about them. When you take people for granted, you assume they will continue doing what you expect them to do.
- Being kind to others does not negate taking them for granted. You must be consistent and treat people with respect.
- You can promote a culture of not taking each other for granted by fostering open and honest communication.

Delegation

One rewarding aspect of realizing our influence is the feeling we get when we can delegate a task or decision to others. There should, however, be an almost equal amount of reward for the person being delegated to, for they now have power based on the responsibility placed on them through the delegation. Proper delegation means that both the taskmaster and the task-maker will be able to share in the potential reward of the results, or they may share the consequences if the task is not delegated or performed properly.

There is always a taskmaster and a task-maker in a delegation scenario. The person who delegates is the taskmaster, and the person receiving the delegation is the task-maker. It is the taskmaster's responsibility to prepare the task-maker. If you fail to prepare the task-maker for their responsibility in what has been delegated, you fail in your responsibility. Remember the example I shared earlier with the hiring process of Lloyd and Harry? This is one of the most common issues in environments where people have been given authority without thought or context of that authority.

For example, pretend there is someone in your office who has amazing technical skills, and this person has been a task-maker for a period of time. Through their positive influence, they then become a taskmaster (a leader). As they begin to delegate the tasks that they once completed, they fail to understand the context of the tasks. This may be due to a lack of current focus on that task and knowing the task so well; they take their own knowledge of the task for granted.

When delegated tasks are not properly explained, the new task-maker may make mistakes or even fail. This is where you may begin to see an overreaction as the taskmaster blames their task-maker. If you choose to delegate something, you still own that decision and result. It was your responsibility to begin with, and it will remain your responsibility no matter who completes the work. You must recognize your responsibility in that delegation and work to rectify the issue instead of deflecting the problem to protect your position.

Delegation is a powerful tool that can be amazingly positive in the hands of a positive leader. It can even be a large component of making an effective leader. This is the only way to keep a growing enterprise moving forward; proper delegation can eliminate the need for multitasking and allow each team member to focus on their tasks with clarity. Additionally, whether we are delegating or being delegated to, it offers us an opportunity to learn.

The key to successful delegation is understanding the full value of it. You can ask yourself, "Does my delegation help teach the task-maker? Am I delegating with confidence? Am I delegating to receive help and to help the task-maker grow, or am I delegating to be selfish and get rid of a task I don't want? Am I willing to accept responsibility for the task and help the task-maker learn if there are mistakes?" If you don't delegate to teach, grow, or get some help, or if you don't trust your team's capabilities, you may fall into the trap of becoming a micromanager. If you micromanage your business and team, you will ultimately fail in the areas that are detrimental to long-term success.

Hence, one of the most dangerous traits of a leader is micromanagement. For example, this can occur when the taskmaster delegates to the task-maker and then hovers over them to ensure the work is completed within certain parameters and to a certain standard. At that point, it would be more productive for the taskmaster to complete the work themselves. When I enter a client's company and identify micromanagers, I can also identify the immense impact of negative issues related to micromanagement, which include cultural issues, high turnover, lack of focus caused by multitasking, and a tremendous lack of respect. These are all things that are exacerbated by a micromanaging taskmaster.

Micromanagers are often born from a need to be in control, which can come from many places. One of the most common sources I have seen is that micromanaging is a learned trait. Those who work with micromanagers often feel that to be a proper leader, they too need to micromanage and take control. Even if someone doesn't work directly with or under a micromanager, traits can rub off on other team members who observe micromanaging behavior from a team leader. Another common way micromanagers are born is through failure. Those who fail may feel a need to buckle down and take more control in order to avoid failures in the future. It can also be born from an inability to trust others, which could stem from one's ego (thinking they are the best at everything) or past relationships (someone has let them down before). Micromanaging tendencies can also come from anxiety, a wish to be recognized for effort, and so much more.

Therefore, how you manage delegation, and micromanaging tendencies if you have them, can be the tipping point in your ability to be an effective leader and influencer within your organization. If you delegate work or a decision to a task-maker, and then are constantly questioning or challenging the authority you gave with that delegation, you are damaging the task-maker's position in the company and their autonomy (their ability to learn and perform the task on their own). Furthermore, you are teaching them negative lessons by creating a scenario where you are either delegating work that you could have done yourself, or you do not respect or trust them enough to complete the task.

There can be other unintended consequences of delegation, like taking someone for granted. When we delegate certain tasks consistently to one person or department on a regular basis, we can fall into the habit of expectation, which can lead us to take them for granted. This type of delegation also leads to assumptions assuming they will always complete that task—which can lead to overreactions if they don't complete it. Delegation can be a pitfall, but it doesn't always have to be. Positive delegation, done in the spirit of being the "I" in team, can be one of the most powerful tools to allow you and your organization to grow.

One of the telltale signs that delegation is becoming a pitfall is when you delegate without any thought at all. There should be a conscious train of thought for each task delegated. The taskmaster must always provide clear direction to the task-maker for all delegated tasks. Delegation requires immense trust on both sides; trust from the taskmaster to the task-maker to perform, and trust from the task-maker to the taskmaster to be set up for success in the task. As a leader, you have a responsibility to follow up and provide support if needed. Keep open lines of communication to allow the task-maker to come to you for questions, and trust that if they have questions or need you, they will come and ask.

Additionally, delegation should not be a flippant decision made to get something off your plate without thought to the responsibility given to the task-maker. Delegating requires that you not only consider the task at hand but that you also consider the task-maker's skills. If the task-maker does not already possess the proper skills, knowledge, or training for the task, you may unknowingly dump a pile of anxiety onto them as they may begin to feel they aren't capable of the task (yet most won't tell you this). As a leader, you need to pair up the task with someone who has the foundation to complete that task. It may require a little guidance and education from you, but they should be prepared to take on such a task. Otherwise, you set them and that task up for failure.

Another aspect of delegation that can be taken for granted is the thought that if you delegate to a task-maker, that task is no longer your responsibility. All delegation is a temporary transfer of the tasks or decisions; however, you only lend the responsibility, not the consequences. You must understand and accept the risks that go with lending your responsibility to the task-maker. If you don't have issues accepting the accolades that come from completing a task, even if that task was delegated, you shouldn't have any issues accepting the consequences. It would be disingenuous and hypocritical to try to deflect the responsibility of consequences to the task-maker if you are fine with accepting the praise as the taskmaster.

Part of owning your choice to delegate a task is not taking for granted the results of that task. You must always account for what could go wrong when you decide to delegate a task and choose whether those risks are worth it. Delegating tasks to your team gives them a positive experience to help them grow by learning new aspects of the company, providing a helping hand, and even opening the door to new opportunities. There are always risks when delegating, but to be a positive leader, you must think through the pros and cons of delegating a task. As a result, you must stand behind the positive or negative outcomes of your delegation.

If the tasks you delegate turn into something positive, then you are giving yourself and your team a positive environment and culture to thrive in. If the tasks you delegate have a negative outcome, you can work with your team to see what happened and where it went wrong to prevent the issue from happening again in the future. The issue might stem from poor communication about the task, the task-maker not having a complete understanding of how to perform the task, or some variation or other off-the-wall issue that can and will occur. Remember to have open communication to identify where and what went wrong. Communication is key to moving any team forward with positivity.

As you should know by now, I tend to delegate to a fault. One of the biggest challenges I have is that I push to grow personally and as an organization very quickly. To accomplish this, I push those around me to perform at a higher level; I never intend to push past someone's ability, but sometimes I fail in this effort. My biggest failure is usually when I delegate my own tasks to others without contemplating what that might do to their already busy schedules.

My tendency to over-delegate means that new team members may get the impression that I take my team for granted, if I were not so insistent that they understand it is my biggest fault as a leader. I am open about delegation, and I ask our team to push back if I begin to take their time or expertise for granted. Part of my fault comes from the fact that I completely trust my team and their capabilities.

Yet there are times when my team doesn't perform the tasks delegated to them as well as I would have hoped. There are even times when it goes horribly wrong. It's important to remember that failure is nothing more than a learning opportunity for everyone involved. Humans tend to overreact when things don't go as expected or when they are in high-stress environments. If you feel negative emotions toward your task-maker for not completing the delegated task up to par, do not allow your emotions to pique. When you overreact to things you can learn from, you can create massive pitfalls for your entire team.

Key Takeaways: Delegation

- There is always a taskmaster and a task-maker in a delegation scenario. The person who delegates is the taskmaster, and the person receiving the delegation is the task-maker.

- The most important part of delegation is communication. If you don't correctly communicate the task and expectations, the task-maker could assume to fill in the gaps of context and make mistakes/fail.
- Another pitfall of delegation is micromanagement. If you're going to micromanage, don't delegate. You're just wasting time and energy.
- You should consciously delegate tasks. This allows you to communicate them effectively and understand the influence you have over the task-maker.
- The task-maker should have the skills, knowledge, or training to successfully handle the task; otherwise, you need to take the time to get them up to speed if you think this task must be delegated to them.
- You must always account for what could go wrong when you decide to delegate a task and choose whether those risks are worth it. Ultimately, you maintain responsibility over the tasks you delegate.

Overreaction

I like to call overreactions a "compound pitfall." Meaning that when there is an overreaction, it is usually triggered by another pitfall that can escalate an already difficult situation into something far more negative. I don't mean to imply that a situation needs to be negative for there to be an overreaction. There can be overreactions to positive situations too. So why *do* we overreact?

Some overreactions are good, or at least okay, while others are not so good. For example, a positive overreaction might occur when you feel so elated that you can't help but react by squealing, jumping, or even happy crying. Some of our most common overreactions are responses to common issues. Overreaction can come from timing, a series of circumstances, a surprise interaction, or even when we lack proper context, leading us to make assumptions about motive or intent.

At IA, we had a client who was extremely insecure about his competition. One day, he saw one of his best employees talking to an employee of his competitor. Our client, who was insecure and under some pressure due to the rivalry between these two firms, lost his temper the next day and degraded this employee in front of several other employees. The employee decided he didn't deserve to be treated that way and promptly quit.

What our client didn't know was that his employee had been long-time friends with the other person, and it was just by chance that his friend had become employed by the competition. In fact, they were meeting because the other company was pressuring the friend to convince our client's employee to leave his company and come work for them—because he was one of the best salespeople on the team.

The compound issue here is clear: Our client lost one of his best salespeople because of his choice to overreact. While we have already covered several ways to understand the responsibility of our influence and bring some balance to our life, overreaction is another byproduct of imbalance. Had our client slowed down, opened a path of communication with his employee, and acted in a responsible manner, he could have understood the full context of the events and reacted more objectively. Again, we don't know what we don't know.

Similarly, the employee could have had a better reaction to his employer's outburst. Rather than quitting, knowing that his employer was insecure about that specific competitor, he could have chosen to take the high road and diffuse the situation. However, he also overreacted, walking away from a job he loved and was good at.

When we overreact to events, especially in a team environment, we can damage the continuity of the team. Some of us may think that our team already knows about our tendency to overreact. That may be true, but even so, our teams are likely to be apprehensive around us for fear of such an outburst. People who are constantly overreacting are hard to be around, as others fear they could be walking on thin ice. This tension doesn't elicit the best out of our teams.

People who overreact tend to influence others in negative ways more than positive ones. People who overact believe their aggression yields results because it motivates others to do what they want. There is a residual price to pay, though, and it is a pitfall. The teams around these people will learn not to be forthcoming, out of fear, or avoid things that cause overreactions. This leads to having a team that isn't willing to take chances on anything.

Overreactions can spill over into your personal life, too. They can extinguish the drive in the people around you for taking chances, being vulnerable, trying new things, and getting more involved. The other problem with overreactions is that you may be influencing others to act in the same way. If you overreact to get your way, regardless of the price, others may mimic the behavior, such as your children, spouse, friends, or co-workers. This does not create a positive influence in the world.

There are many ways to deal with overreactions, but I find the best method is to confront the behavior. When you can develop trust in communication, you relinquish the need to overreact. By developing trust, you create an environment where people don't feel the need to lash out to get their point across. People will feel content knowing they are being listened to, and this will ease the impulse to overreact. Setting these parameters for how you communicate with others is vital, and you must understand how people on your team communicate in order to reduce overreactions.

Determining what qualifies as an overreaction can be subjective. Most of the topics we discuss in life are subjective to our perception of the world; there is no cookie-cutter way to discuss any of the topics we discuss in this series. However, we *know* when we overreact, and others know it too. It is our responsibility to know our environment, especially if we are on a team. While a regular reaction by one person may be an overreaction for another, it's important to remember our setting.

Fortunately, there are some settings where overreacting isn't bad or negative. My wife, René, may be one of the most positive people I know. When she is happy, she shows it. Happiness for her often seems like an overreaction, and it's infectious for those of us who know her. However, this can be viewed as negative by those who do not know her or do not know people *like* her. Sometimes people assume that nobody could possibly be that friendly, excited, or happy, and they view her actions as overreacting. They are wrong, because there are people in the world, like René, who *are* that happy, and part of the joy they feel is in their expression of joy.

Some of you may be curious as to why some people are put off by those who exude joy. Unfortunately, it's often the negativity in their own lives. Their negative reaction to positivity is, itself, an overreaction. They take for granted that there are people who still act or overreact to positive life events. They may feel that others should be as miserable as they are. Nobody needs to feel this way, which is another reason why being a positive influence is so powerful.

If you overreact and catch yourself, the best thing you can do is to be upfront about it. Just like when you make a mistake, the best way to rectify it is to be honest, have open communication, and do your best to fix it. You can apologize to those affected and ask yourself why you overreacted. Ultimately, the way to reduce overreaction is to get to the root cause of what triggered it, such as fear in the client example I shared. When you can identify your mistakes as you make them, you move closer to conquering its source.

For example, if we take something or someone for granted, we may create a pitfall and set ourselves up for an overreaction if things do not occur as expected—we overreact to the change. We can be left feeling disappointed, hurt, surprised, or angry, and those surprise feelings can make us overreact if we were expecting the situation to go a different way. In a changing world, and with how complicated we are as humans, it's unrealistic to assume that things or people will always be a certain way. We must avoid these pitfalls in order to increase our positive influence.

Key Takeaways: Overreaction

- By overreacting, you can instill fear or anxiety in your team. They may not feel comfortable being honest with you out of fear you will overreact.
- If you overreact and catch yourself, the best thing you can do is to be upfront about it. Just like when you make a mistake, the best way to rectify an overreaction is to be honest, have open communication, and do your best to fix it.

World Influence

Let's start by identifying the phrase "world influence" by its many other names and phrases: Karma, reap what you sow, the law of attraction, divine will, chance, destiny, you get what you deserve, and many others. Whether you believe in any of these approaches or just believe that all things happen at random, our point for this section is that negative occurrences are often a pitfall resulting from your actions. As we have stated several times, your influence is your greatest responsibility. It's up to you to decide if you put out a negative or positive influence into the world, but you must know that the energy you put out (the influence you put out) comes back to you.

This is the universe's way of balancing the actions and decisions we make as humans. It's okay if you don't believe in this power of influence specifically. While I believe there is a balancing that happens in the universe, and I personally choose to call it karma, there is a way to frame it that can reach all of our beliefs: The lens of influence. The influence we put out and then receive back tends to happen at random—it either does or does not happen. Returned influence is not always guaranteed, and even then, it could happen weeks, months, or even years after the occurrence. I believe our actions in life create opportunities for other actions, like cause and effect. When our actions are repaid to us, that is typically our influence reflecting back. Another way to describe this is the law of attraction: If you think or act in a negative or positive way, you will attract negative or positive occurrences.

An example that comes up in my life quite regularly is getting a great parking spot. René is an amazingly good-hearted person, so whenever we go out shopping together, we somehow always get an amazing parking spot. It may seem small, but sometimes it's the little things that can bring us the most joy—especially when you live in the Midwest in the winter. However, whenever I am out shopping alone, I never get a great parking spot. I attribute this to René being so kind and open that the universe is rewarding her positive influence with short walks to our destination.

There are some who will say this is by chance, or something else entirely. Regardless of the "cause," I believe there is something higher at play around us, and the positive or negative energies we put into the world have an effect one way or another. Something as simple as getting a close parking spot becomes something that reinforces positive behavior. No matter how we choose to label this, it creates more positive influence. More importantly, there is nothing negative about celebrating a positive occurrence. Sometimes, it's the little things in life that add to our positivity.

There may be people in your life who seem to have everything figured out—they have money, a good job, a happy marriage or partner, many friends, and more. However, there is not a single human alive who does not have some sort of negativity in their life. How we choose to *respond* to that negativity sets us apart from others. Our choice to respond positively will not only change our perception of life but can change what life gives back to us and those we influence.

However, when negative things occur in life out of the blue, I use it as a moment to reflect on my influence and what I have been giving the world. Just like with the close parking spot, negative occurrences show me I may not have been living up to my best potential. Instead of getting a reward (positive influence), I receive a punishment (negative influence). I enjoy this way of thinking because it eliminates blame and justification. I'm not looking for a simple excuse when something negative happens to me; in fact, it's quite the opposite. I use it as an opportunity to identify areas of my life where I may need to improve. When something good happens to me, I feel satisfied and rewarded for doing good things.

Additionally, I want to clarify that I don't assume everything that happens to me is due to my influence. I recognize that there are moments in life that are completely by chance and that not everything relates to how we think and act. However, by living with the mindset that what we put out is what we receive back, a positive or negative occurrence makes me think. It allows me to reflect on my actions, look for areas of improvement, and helps me grow.

Believing in the power of influence and seeing the energy in the world around me has had a profound effect on my way of thinking. It encourages me to be a positive influence and a better person. Not because I fear negative retribution, but because I don't even want to put negativity out into the world to begin with. I readily accept accountability and never shy away from accepting whatever occurs as the result of an action I am responsible for. I have my bad days, but I still strive to be a positive influence every day. When I make mistakes, I work hard to rectify those mistakes to the best of my ability in order to re-balance the situation (and hopefully keep my influence balanced as well). If I fail to bring full balance back into the situation, the universe's influence will bring balance back itself.

Influence has a way of re-balancing a situation that has been thrown off, but not in a "tit for tat" or "eye for an eye" kind of way. I am going to refer to my parking spot example, as I am sure this has happened to all of you. One time, I witnessed a person waiting to pull into a parking spot. While they were waiting patiently, with their turn signal on, for the person to back out, another car sped up and stole the spot from them. The person waiting did not get angry; they had a look of disappointment, while the person who stole the spot looked smug.

About 30 or 40 minutes later, I was back in the parking lot. I noticed a police car parked in the aisle where this spot stealing occurred because there had been an accident. The person who had stolen the parking spot had, in their rush to leave, backed into someone else's car. Call it karma, chance, or whatever you want—I believe the accident occurred to balance out this person's reckless, selfish, and unkind actions. But why? How?

Some may think that stealing a parking spot and then getting into a fender-bender isn't "fair" and that it would ultimately create more imbalance. In reality, we don't know what other negativity this person was conducting or if the person they hit was also creating negativity. Perhaps they were in a rush, or maybe they just didn't care. Nevertheless, I wish I knew the person who was hit; as it happens, I knew the kid who was driving the car and stole the spot. Later, we discussed the whole event and his actions, and I learned that he described himself as having "bad luck."

It all happened because he didn't slow down. It started with a speeding ticket the day of the accident. He was speeding because he was late to be somewhere; then, he was in a hurry to stop at the store to grab something, which prompted him to steal the parking space. He just kept going fast and didn't slow down, which made him rush to leave and back into the car that was waiting behind him to take his spot. He eventually lost his job over being habitually late when he was speeding, again, and got another ticket.

On a positive note, he eventually learned his lesson about rushing and blaming others for his misfortunes. Over the summer, he began to take accountability for his actions and used those negative moments to change his behavior. He started having a positive influence and ultimately earned a job doing exactly what he wanted.

He was able to reach his goals—whatever you want to call it, these experiences influenced him in meaningful ways in the long run.

Lessons learned can have a positive effect to help us change and become better people. Those who regularly see themselves as "unlucky" and fail to try to learn from their experiences are creating a negative influence in our society. I am reminded of a "Twilight Zone" episode where the main character was racist. His rants were a negative influence on those around him; friends began to shy away from him because of his comments. The character is then suddenly dropped into situations where he is himself but is viewed by the world as a person he would degrade and speak poorly about—he is the minority. The show leaves us with the impression that he will spend the remainder of his life in a continual loop of negative lessons.

Those who choose to live a negative life influence their surroundings and perception to remain negative. We all know someone who is pessimistic and trouble seems to follow them. They are all-around bummers, dragging everyone else down with their negativity. They can turn any event, despite positive surroundings, into a negative one, thereby influencing those around them. This doesn't mean that a pessimist can't have a positive influence. How you perceive the world and how you act in the world are two different things. Karma, the law of attraction, divine will, or what have you, will give you what you put out. You can choose to lead a positive or a negative life.

If you are someone who feels like trouble finds you or that you are unlucky, take a step back and think of the negativity as your influence finding its way back to you. If you had negative issues in your past, you could be faced with continued challenges as you learn that lesson. However, if you begin to tackle these lessons and challenges with a positive frame of mind, you can begin to reap the rewards of positivity. If you choose to recognize influence and its role in your life, you open yourself up to other possibilities that maybe things aren't happening *to* you, but they are happening *because* of you. By opening your mind to the possibility that things happen because of your actions, you put yourself in a position to consider your actions and their effects. This goes hand-in-hand with self-accountability.

Within the universe's influence, luck, karma, chance, or however you want to define what happens to you, there are lessons of influence embedded. They are subjective to the person it happens to and objective for those of us watching. How you interpret those situations is also important for how you move forward, grow your positive influence, and accept responsibility for the things you do that may be a negative influence. I am not sure how many people notice when they get an amazing parking spot, but sometimes the little things in life can bring you the most joy.

Key Takeaways: World Influence

- What you put into the world, you receive back. This is called the law of attraction, karma, reaping what you sow, and so much more. When you make space for positivity, you attract positivity.
- Your actions create opportunities for other actions, either from yourself or others. Depending on your actions and teeing up this opportunity for others, the subsequent actions may be positive or negative.
- Nobody has everything figured out. Everyone struggles with something.
- How you perceive the world and how you interact with the world are two different things. Pessimists won't always make you feel negative, and optimists won't always make you feel good.

Happiness

You may be wondering why we have included happiness here in the chapter on pitfalls. For me, I think happiness can get in the way of reality, meaning that when we are happy with our lives or situations, we take things for granted, assume, overreact, get stuck in the status quo, and avoid change or growth. However, my more eloquent daughter Mary has a definition of why happiness can be a pitfall, so I am going to turn this section over to Mary after I leave you with a parting thought:

Happiness is like prosperity. It's subjective according to each person's own interpretation. One person's idea of happiness may be another's idea of misery. Happiness can change; what makes us happy as a child or as an adolescent is different from what makes us happy as an adult. And, as Mary has pointed out to me in her writing, I too believe the search for happiness can be a pitfall.

In our search for happiness, we can do things that may create huge pitfalls in our lives. I will compare this to having intentions. Sometimes we can have the best and most positive intentions, but things don't always go as planned. Even when we have the best intentions, there are times when we will make mistakes and create negative actions through our positive intentions. Now, I will turn the remainder of this section over to Mary. As a young adult, she has learned lessons differently than I and can help bridge the gap between the philosophy and experiences of her generation and those yet to come.

Mary

We strive for happiness as a state of being. We put happiness on a pedestal as the epitome of what our lives *should* reflect. We believe that the people we follow on social media are always happy because of the snippets of their lives we see. We have been raised to believe that if we are not happy, then we are not living to our fullest potential. We frown upon other emotions like sadness, anger, fear, and disgust, and expect that if we feel these things, then we are not living correctly. Happiness is an emotion, just like sadness, anger, fear, and disgust, and it is not a state of being we should constantly strive for—this is why it can become a pitfall.

I wouldn't call this an unpopular opinion so much as an *undiscussed* opinion. However, I will pose a few questions for you to ponder: If someone is so focused on striving for happiness, how much of their life do they miss? Does this fixation leave them with tunnel vision, forcing them to ignore the other pleasures of life? And if they were to fixate on finding happiness and lost sight of the rest of life, what kind of quality of life would that be?

When I was in college, I worked at a counseling center and was privileged to learn from esteemed psychologists, as well as their clients. It was an eye-opening experience into the perceptions and lives of others. We had a rainbow of people come in for sessions, ranging from 3 to 80 years old. Having a peek behind the curtain of hundreds of lives significantly influenced who I am today and many of my life philosophies.

I learned my philosophy on happiness—viewing it as an emotion rather than a state of being—from a psychologist I worked with closely. One day, she said to me, "I don't believe that happiness is a state of being. I believe it is an emotion and it should be reserved as such. I believe *contentment* is a state of being." This one passing comment has stuck with me, and I think about it almost daily. It's one of those things that I have come to truly believe. I believe that if others felt the same, we would all live more fulfilling lives. That is why I have chosen to write this section for you. I want to debunk the happiness pitfall.

When we strive for happiness as a state of being and believe it is possible to be constantly happy, we set ourselves up for failure. It is not possible for emotions to be a constant state. Even when dealing with depression—which I have personally dealt with—there are small twinges and waves of other emotions. I want to be clear that there are always exceptions to the rule; I have seen people suffer from worse depression than me, and I by no means wish to invalidate any of the emotions that anyone feels while dealing with depression. Conversely, because there are exceptions to the rule, like mental illness, no one can possibly live fully immersed in a single emotion at all times.

Nevertheless, emotions are meant to have peaks and valleys, as that is part of our human experience. We are meant to experience happiness, sadness, fear, loathing, regret, and the spectrum of other emotions we all feel on a daily basis. Unfortunately, when we strive for happiness as a state of being, we make it impossible for us to (1) achieve that state and (2) feel other emotions. It's completely improbable to expect that one would always be happy. When we expect this, we begin to take happiness for granted.

If you are constantly striving to be happy—at work, at home, with your friends, in your creative space—how are you to know when you are truly happy? Think of happiness as a little yellow ball. In this hypothetical scenario, assume that you have achieved happiness as your state of being, meaning you are always holding a little yellow ball. If you are always holding a little yellow ball, when do you start to take holding it for granted? At some point, you would begin to assume that you will always be holding that little yellow ball.

Now, let's say you decide to go to your favorite restaurant in the whole world and order your favorite meal. This is an occurrence that would make most people feel happy, joyful, or excited. But not you; you're already holding the little yellow ball and have been for a long time. So, what emotion do you leave room for when you get to go to your favorite restaurant? Most likely, disappointment. However, this simply means that your state of being will be difficult to elevate. In the face of an event that should cause you to feel happy, you have no room to grow because you are in a constant state of happiness.

To live in a constant state of happiness would mean to dull your sensitivity to happiness and make life lackluster. This is not only the opposite of what you were striving for to begin with, but it also makes life boring. By always holding that little yellow ball, life becomes predictable. You begin to take that ball for granted, assuming that you will always be holding it, and you stop striving for things that will make you happy. Why strive for something when you constantly have it?

Therefore, striving to be constantly happy is a pitfall. It's unrealistic, and even in a scenario where you could be happy all the time, it would be counterproductive, as your happiness would begin to lose its appeal while simultaneously making the rest of life appear dull in comparison. Part of the beautiful human experience is immersing yourself in other emotions. While you may not feel good all the time, you must try to have gratitude for those negative emotions, as they remind you of your humanity. Emotions teach you lessons and give you an opportunity to grow and realize that being human is beautiful because of its complexity.

Instead, I believe in striving for a state of contentment. Here I define contentment as feeling secure about where you are in life. Contentment can be seen as feeling at peace with yourself and your place in life. However, I do not mean to say that by feeling content, or that striving for contentment, you cannot also set goals, push your boundaries, succeed and fail, or even strive for that which makes you feel happy. I mean that we should all strive to feel comfortable and neutral in our lives while continuing to push ourselves and others to grow and evolve into better human beings. Striving for a constant state of happiness is impossible and will leave you feeling empty.

Again, when we feel content, we feel centered in who we are, where we are, what we are, and why we are. It also allows us to appreciate and fully immerse ourselves in the emotion of happiness. It becomes a welcomed surprise to feel happy, like a special present we get to hold onto for brief periods of time. We begin to appreciate and have gratitude for the moments when we get to hold that little yellow ball. By striving to feel content in life, we open ourselves up to the flow of emotion that is part of our human experience.

To be a positive influence, we should strive to be content. We should be comfortable knowing that we won't always be happy and accept that. When we can accept life for all its peaks and valleys, we can begin to understand life more clearly. We set ourselves up for success, not failure, when we strive to be content. That success carries on through our influence on ourselves and our team. We can be more realistic and empathetic towards others when we accept this. We can understand emotions more clearly when we allow ourselves to feel them freely, instead of constantly trying to achieve just one of them.

The best advice I have for being content is to practice gratitude. Look around at all the things that you can be grateful for. Think about our basic human needs—food, shelter, clothing, health, love—and be appreciative of having those things. It can sometimes be hard to remember that not everyone is as lucky; there are many people in this world lacking in basic human necessities. Look at what you can be grateful for and decide today that those things are enough to make you content.

Then, set goals for yourself to achieve what you want. I am not saying you have to settle with being content. You can still reach for things that will make you happy and bask in the warmth of that happiness once it is achieved. But happiness is ephemeral, and if you chase it, you will need higher and higher doses to deliver the same high. Instead, you need to strive for growth and achievement and allow those things to make you happy when you do reach them. This will give you a platform on which you can appreciate feeling happy. You can feel gratitude toward the moment you strived for. If you allow happiness to remain an emotion, then you won't feel disappointed or upset when you can't be in its constant state.

Finally, I am under the impression that short-term happiness can be defined as immediate gratification, like eating candy, while long-term happiness is usually more structured and goal oriented. You need both in your life. As long as your actions don't intentionally cause a negative influence-ripple, setting yourself up for happiness is human. Additionally, if you want to share your snippet of happiness with the world on social media because it makes you feel good, do it. Social media seems to be a catalyst for idolizing happiness, and I am not against it. Why shouldn't you share your happiness with the world? It's just important to remember that social media is deceiving in that you see only what people want you to see. Therefore, do not idolize others because of what they seemingly have.

In the end, your life is in your hands, so don't squander it by chasing just one emotion. Don't let your life pass you by without allowing yourself to be fully immersed in the true human experience: love, loss, friendship, work, community, devotion, pleasure, and pain. (And I'm sure there are more I have yet to experience.) Find your contentment and be at peace with yourself. Continue to strive to be the best human you can be, develop yourself, and encourage those around you to do the same.

Key Takeaways: Happiness

- Happiness is subjective. You need to define what happiness means to you based on your perspective.
- Happiness is an emotion, just like sadness, anger, fear, and disgust. It is not a state of being to be constantly strived for—this is why it can become a pitfall. Believing happiness is a state of being rather than an emotion sets you up for failure.
- Living in a constant state of happiness means to dull your sensitivity to happiness and make life lackluster. This is not only the opposite of what you were striving for to begin with (happiness), but it also makes life boring.
- Strive for contentment. Feel at peace with yourself and your place in life, and don't stop reaching for things that will bring you joy. Treat happiness as a fleeting emotion, like all the others, while maintaining contentment.

- Practice gratitude by thinking about the basic human needs—food, shelter, clothing, health, love—and appreciating that you have those things.

Pitfalls Reflection

Unfortunately, avoiding pitfalls is tricky; we may find ourselves on a path laden with them as we step carefully to avoid each one. We will definitely fall into some, but it's how we get out and move on from the fall that defines our influence as leaders. Learning from our mistakes is what helps us grow as people. It's what helps our teams grow. If we can equate pitfalls to mistakes, then pitfalls are just springboards for opportunity when handled the right way. To increase our positive influence, we must look for pitfalls *and* help those around us who have fallen into them.

CHAPTER 4
CHANGE

> **"It is not the strongest of the species that survive, nor the most intelligent, but the one most responsive to change."**
> **—Charles Darwin**

Change is one thing we can rely on to be consistent in this world, for things are always shifting and moving. Change can be planned, forced, anticipated, or a surprise. We change—whether in significant or minuscule ways—every time we read something or take in new information. To take it a step further, influence is what initiates change, meaning that all change *begins* with influence.

Influence comes in a myriad of different ways and can be misused or misunderstood. A hot, overused title today is "influencer," which we could easily call "changer" and it would have the same meaning. Influencers have one goal: To change the way you perceive, think, or perform. Sometimes that change is intended for your benefit, and sometimes it is for the benefit of others. Typically, however, these "influencers" are just in business to create change for themselves, and they use the title to give others the impression that they are superior. But that is not the case. As I hope you believe by now, each of us has a powerful influence. No matter how unknown you are, or how popular you are, your influence matters.

Change is the goal of the *"I" in Team* series. To be honest, writing has been therapeutic, and the habit has been good for me. I have learned about myself and the people around me; I have altered my views and grown in my positive influence by working on this series, and I hope the same for everyone who reads it. For me, writing allows me to slow down and think more deeply about the topics and subjects on my mind at that moment. Having the opportunity to slow down, think deeply, and become mindful has changed my approach in quite a few situations. I believe this stems from the *practice* of slowing down and being mindful, since you become better at anything you practice. If you didn't know this already, making a new habit for yourself creates change in your life.

Change is not something to shy away from. Change brings new beginnings and is something we can, and should, embrace. We see change everywhere, not just in our personal and professional lives but around the world. In politics, stories, sides, and positions are changing constantly. In marketing, businesses use strategies to alter public perception regarding their products. To give you an example of this, one of the most notable changes I have seen in the advancement of marketing throughout my lifetime was with the Cadillac. I was born in the 1960s and raised in the 1970s and 1980s. During this time, middle-aged individuals, like my grandfather and his peers, bought Cadillacs. In the 1990s, Cadillac began introducing models that were sleeker and geared toward a younger generation.

What ended up happening was that the same generation bought them in the hope of feeling younger, as opposed to the company's intended outcome of a younger generation buying them.

There was a slow shift in the 2000s, but the real change in the Cadillac branding strategy became apparent to me in the 2010s. I noticed some of my friends in their 40s buying Cadillacs instead of a Mercedes or BMW. This was partially fueled by a movement to "buy American." In 2016, I noticed younger individuals in their 30s buying Cadillac. My own son, just turning 16, expressed an interest in them—something I never would have done when I was 16. Cadillac has indeed successfully marketed to a younger generation, and I see it everywhere as younger individuals are driving them. This is just one observation of change in the consumer market. The same can be said for plant-based products, e-cigarettes, and more. Buying habits and patterns are constantly changing.

While not all of them have a tremendous impact, these changes do transform the way our society perceives the world over time. How we deal with change significantly alters how others perceive our influence. In fact, observing change in organizations is the reason I became a business advisor. I became fascinated with the effects of change on people, personally and professionally. We are evolving creatures and have opportunities to change almost daily.

If we ask people their opinions on change, I believe that most would say they don't like, or maybe even hate, change. However, we have been faced with change our entire lives. From the moment we were born, we began taking in information, and that information has changed us, little by little, to make us into the people we are today. As we continue to be influenced, we continue to change. We are all in a constant state of personal evolution. That is not to say we are all in a state of *positive* evolution, but we are all still changing.

When we consciously think about change, our minds tend to turn it into a negative. We fear change, as it is the unknown. Alas, change is inevitable. So, we must accept that change is consistent. The challenge is to find a way to consciously embrace change in a pragmatic way, so we can be positively influenced by the unknown. Only by opening ourselves up to the possibility of change will we learn, grow, and become positive leaders for ourselves and our teams.

All change begins with a choice.

Choice and Decision

Sometimes it can be hard to make seemingly simple decisions. If your choices for breakfast are between an apple and a banana, that's a simple decision (for most). If you're deciding whether to move to Spain for a year, that may not be so simple. If you previously committed to something that was the wrong decision for you, you can harbor negative emotions toward that experience and begin to doubt your ability to choose.

You begin with choices in front of you, but a decision requires electing just one of those choices. Decision and choice are quite similar, but choice comes before decision. Choice is theoretical, while decision is final and concrete. Decisions are what commit us to changing our future; they imply that we have analyzed the differences between our "once were" choices. If you're ready to make a change in your life, that means you have a decision coming up. One of the best ways to find the choices to inform your decision is through research (if the choices are not already presented to you, or if you want to know if there are any additional choices). Research and communicate with others who have made similar decisions. For example, the decision to go to school. Do you want in-person or online classes? Do you want to attend a university or community college? In what field do you want to obtain a degree? Find people who have made a similar decision and pick their brains to understand how they found the choices available to them.

Unfortunately, I believe the prospect of change makes deciding between choices and finding additional choices incredibly difficult for some. Every time we make a decision, we are choosing how to influence change. Choice can drift into a sensitive area for some topics; there are always exceptions to choice that are confined by laws, mental health, physical health, and more (I do not wish to defend or be a proponent of any social or political arguments in this section in relation to choice). For example, considering company policies, there are times when we may need to follow regulations. We may not feel we have a choice in certain situations because of the rules or laws we live with; however, living or working within these areas is still a choice.

There are positions in life that may limit the choices available to you, and these types of positions are typically confined by mental and physical health. I recently read a story about the CEO of a company who put a symbol on his company uniforms that conflicted with several individuals' personal beliefs. They then had to make a choice regarding working for the company. If the industry had mandated such a requirement, meaning that to participate in the overall industry, one must wear a symbol, then those people would have not only had to make a choice but a *decision* on their overall career choices.

There are also socioeconomic positions where choice is diminished. For example, if you don't have the money to pursue a decision you want to make, your socioeconomic status hinders your ability to make that decision. To those who are experiencing a life where your power to choose is captive, I believe you still have a choice in how you use your influence to empower yourself and the people closest to you, including your community. There will always be times in life when you don't have the power to choose, but I urge you to look at these moments as exceptions. We will be discussing the freedom of decision here and how to use it in tandem with your positive influence.

When you are faced with a choice, begin by contemplating what you believe is moral and ethical, define your values, and move forward in your decision-making process with an understanding of each choice you have. You may also take into consideration how your decision will influence those around you. No matter the decision you make, there will be accountability involved. People will be influenced by your decision, and it's best to prepare yourself for what might come from that. There are times when your decisions will disrupt the balance of things and bring consequences, intended or unintended. Think about your choices carefully and imagine their outcomes.

To give you an example of choice and the consequences of decisions, I have a dramatic example. I was driving home after a Colorado Avalanche hockey game, and traffic coming out of the stadium was heavy as I was attempting to merge onto I-25. In front of me were two cars full of people who seemed to be in a heated argument. Even as we got out of traffic and made it onto the highway, they stayed close to each other. Suddenly, a full can of beer was thrown out of one car intending to hit the other car, but it bounced off that car and hit the front of my truck.

I wasn't happy about a random object striking my truck, but I decided to stay where I was and not get involved. That is, until a tire iron came flying out of the car a few minutes later. That tire iron hit the other car—mind you, while we were still driving down the highway at 60 miles per hour—bounced off that car again and came spiraling onto my windshield, splintering the entire thing like a spiderweb.

Now, I was pissed. My truck had been struck twice, with the last shattering my windshield. This is when I decided to get involved since one car ducked behind the other to tailgate them. I followed suit and called 911. While I was talking to the dispatcher, I continued to follow the two cars, who went back and forth between playing chicken and trying to escape.

Once we had traveled to the back roads of Denver, in the middle of nowhere with no streetlights, the dispatcher informed me that a sheriff's deputy was coming up behind me. I was told to stay in my car and pull over to the side to avoid being in the way. Well, it wasn't just one officer behind me. Suddenly, five or six police cars were blocking the road ahead and to the sides, with their lights flipped on.

The deputy behind me ran up to my car window and reinforced, "Stay in your car." As he walked away, he lifted his AR-15 and approached the other two vehicles. The scene was pure chaos. There were cops everywhere, all with their guns out. They were swarming the two cars, screaming at everyone to stay where they were. They pulled the passengers out one by one, and not one of them put their guns down while doing it.

About 20 minutes later, I was finally asked by an officer if I was okay and if I would follow them to the sheriff's department to make a statement. At the station, I told them the story in full, and they took pictures of the damage to my truck: My windshield, headlight, and turn signal. Then they dropped this statement on me: "You saved a man's and a woman's life."

Our decisions have a ripple effect, even if we don't know it in the moment. The man whose life I apparently saved had been driving with his wife and was pissed at the guys in the other car for some unknown reason. However, the guys in the other car were in a gang. As the man and his wife escalated the situation, the gang of four guys, all with loaded guns, decided to act. The guns were out and ready, and the police believed they intended to kill the couple. Someone had previously called 911 and provided a license plate number after seeing guns in the car. When I called later and provided the same license plate number, the police knew what they were getting into.

With freedom of choice comes people who will attempt to influence your decision. Those who are trying to influence the decisions you make may state subtle phrases such as, "Don't overthink it" or "Make up your mind." The man whose life I saved tried to change the judge's decision to pay for the damages to my truck, stating that I shouldn't have been so nosy as to have followed them so closely anyway. Statements such as these are meant to speed up or alter your decision-making process for the sake of their own impatience. As I always teach, slow down your decision-making process. In the end, your decision will influence you in the present and in the future, as well as the present and future of all those involved.

There will be times when you think you have made a definitive decision and you begin to second-guess yourself. Second-guessing your decisions may come from your current environment and may affect your ability to choose. Change can happen in subtle ways, meaning our perception from day to day can change based on a number of factors. In these times, remember your foundation, morals and ethics, and values to ensure you are contemplating change from your viewpoint.

There have been times in my life, mostly when I was a teen, when I made decisions that I am not proud of. Upon years of reflection and acceptance, I understand and empathize with my past self, and I do not regret any of them. I do wish my decisions had been better and that they didn't have a negative influence on others. However, I believe that it is highly unlikely that if I had lived my life any differently, I would be where I am today; and I would not want my life to be any different today.

It's a cliché, but hindsight truly is 20/20. We simply don't know what we don't know—until it happens. In 1994, my career was complicated and often sporadic, on top of trying to balance work with life. On the work side, there were periods of helping several clients and then none. At the time, my approach toward clients was immature and my understanding of my clients' uniqueness was underdeveloped. On the life side, I had just tried out for some major-league baseball teams and was invited to Spring Training, so I spent time with personal trainers in order to prepare myself. In addition to all this, my wife René was in her third trimester with Mary.

I was pretty excited about the potential opportunity to play baseball again, and the consequence of this was that I put more energy into preparing for baseball than I did into the work structure I had created for myself. My work structure was typically very organized, regardless of how many clients I had at the time. I had a schedule and it helped me stay on track. However, my excitement at a potential life change to do something I loved propelled me to abandon this known structure to engage in something far more disorganized. If I had known at the time how important this structure was to my work, I wouldn't have lost sight of it in favor of my personal pursuits, but we don't know what we don't know. Unfortunately, my newfound disorganized way of doing my work lost me my largest client at the time.

Then, Mary was born early via emergency cesarean, and I was not ready. In the midst of training and having just lost my largest client, we suddenly had a newborn. I had no control over where I worked or who I would be working for. The culmination of these decisions led me to a point of desperation that put me on a highway during a time when I typically wouldn't have been there. As a result, I was hit by a drunk driver. They smashed into the back of my 1988 Ford Bronco II going roughly 40 miles per hour.

The effects of this accident influenced our lives dramatically. I had to slow down due to my injuries, at a time when slowing down wasn't even in my vocabulary like it is today. I had to focus on the way I completed tasks and communicated while I endured 3 wrist surgeries and a jaw splint for traumatic TMJ for 18 months. During this time, we learned that newborn Mary had a life-threatening medical issue. Needless to say, it was an overwhelming time in my life that, upon reflection, wasn't wholly caused through my choices but had I made different ones would have gone much differently. I had no control over someone being drunk behind the wheel, but I *did* have control over how much effort and time I put into my clients. My work/life balance was lost, and the decision to be imbalanced culminated to this chaotic point.

Our luck changed again in October 1995 when the insurance companies settled my case. At this time, I started focusing on my work with a new and refreshed mind. That accident—which, at the time, seemed to be terrible luck with no silver lining—became the catalyst for what we have done to influence the world up to today.

I can say with clarity that there has been a plethora of events born out of the influence of that accident, which would not have, most likely, happened without that accident. I know this from my personal self-reflection, which I wrote about in the first book.

When we deal with the negative consequences of choice and decision, of course we wish it could be different. Naturally, I wish that the pain I went through with my car accident had happened differently. When I look back at some of my life's greatest changes, most of those changes have been directly linked to decisions I made. Currently, I enjoy reflecting on these moments as they give me greater clarity into my decision-making process. I try to learn from my choices and turn negative influence into opportunities and advantages.

There must be times in your life that automatically come to mind when you think of choices you've had and decisions you've made that have affected you in a dramatic way, or even less than dramatic ways; they had an influence on you that was memorable. How can you be deliberate in action and decision-making, in the face of the unknown, to avoid negative consequences? My greatest piece of advice to you is to slow down. There are few negative consequences to taking extra time to make decisions, but there are exceptions, like a hard deadline.

By slowing down, you can bring clarity to a decision. Time removes the need to be impulsive but also allows you to find your concrete decision so there is no holding back or second-guessing. The risks and rewards of your decisions are subjective based on your perceptions. As you slow down and work through a decision, you can use the S.M.A.R.T. (specific, measurable, attainable, realistic, timely) method to help analyze the choices in front of you. Ask questions like, "What factors are driving my decision-making process? Do I feel rushed to make this decision? Are any of these choices aligned with my current goals? Have I considered the positive and negative aspects of each choice? Which negative am I willing to live with?" Additionally, bouncing ideas around with a friend might prove quite useful; but ultimately, the decision is yours to make alone, and nobody can help you do that.

Slowing down influences us in a positive way; it can prevent us from falling into the pitfall of immediate gratification (another pitfall we did not discuss in this book, but discussed in the first book). The issue with allowing ourselves immediate gratification is that it is intellectually lazy. Meaning, we don't even consider the consequences of our actions. This breeds further need for immediate gratification. Slowing down is the means by which we can determine if the choices we have will lead to potential success or regret. Only by knowing ourselves fully and understanding who we want to be can we make the best decisions.

Our first defense against making hasty decisions is to ask ourselves this question: "What are the negative consequences of taking some extra time to make this decision?" This will slow us down. Most of the negative influence we pass onto others stems from a poorly analyzed or hasty decision. If we magnify the slowing-down process of decision-making, what does that look like? To magnify the slowing-down process of our decision-making means that we must focus on it.

Due Diligence

First, we cannot completely focus on something if we are multitasking. Our first objective is to become 100 percent focused on the choice at hand. Then, we should ask if there is anything about the situation that we don't have enough information about. To do so, we will have to review the choices and areas where we may feel we lack an understanding. This will help bring to light all the facts of the choices we are deciding between, giving us the ability to make a more informed decision. Stay focused on the context at hand.

If we are making a huge life decision and need to stay organized in the process, we should not be afraid to write things down. Keep a flowchart, sticky notes, or just a piece of paper nearby to jot down any extra ideas that come floating around. One of the dangers of the learning process is that while we may be focused on learning one thing, we may realize there are other things we don't know about and shift our attention. We may fall into a trap where we begin to focus on this new topic and forget our previous topic. Then, we are missing information as we become unfocused. Keeping ourselves organized will help us tremendously.

I have an example of this magnification process gone awry. One of our clients came to us about helping them with an acquisition. They wanted to acquire a competitor that was growing and doing well. The two partners were very excited about the prospect of joining together once they understood the influence both companies would have on the market. They truly got along well.

When my firm was brought in to assist with the acquisition, the two partners were giddy over the prospect of their combined companies. On paper, the acquisition looked good. Both sides, however, had people telling them to slow down, look at the financials in greater detail, and dig further into how the combined operations were going to run. Yes, on the surface, it appeared to be a nearly perfect fit.

After the companies merged, initially, there was a lot of positive feedback from the market and the teams. Then the fractures began to show. First, prior to the acquisition, the salespeople from each company had highlighted the perceived negatives of each other's offerings and companies to their clients. These previously communicated negatives began to cause credibility issues for the combined firm. Then, one of the company's debts was called due. It was the type of debt that had a balloon, meaning that the entirety of the balance was due all at once, and this put a strain on the company and the relationship between the two new partners.

Finally, the two companies had different cultures and personalities; while the partners were very similar, the way they ran their companies was quite different as the employees were *not* similar.

These subtle differences influenced the partners and their subordinates to make decisions that were contributing to deeper fractures.

Unfortunately, IA's involvement in the merger excluded us from performing due diligence, which is something we would typically always perform during a merger. For example, we would normally verify all financial statements and the backgrounds of both companies, as well as gathering information about the cultures and people. This would have allowed us to fully analyze the people, process, and technology of the two companies to ensure the merger had proceeded in a smoother manner. Instead, we played solely a supporting role in the discussions between just the partners. Our recommendation to slow down was overshadowed by the giddiness of the opportunity and potential these firms had in the markets they served from a financial perspective. They dismissed the impact and influence that the individual people and culture would have on future operations and the market itself.

Like in all mergers and acquisitions, had these two partners done due diligence (research) prior to making this decision, they could have identified their differences and put actions in place to rectify them. For example, since each company's culture was so distinct, we could have facilitated assessments prior to the merger and conducted team-building activities that would have created a stronger bond. When we deal with issues up front, we face fewer surprises later. These issues could have been worked out, or the two businesses could have decided to remain competitors.

In choices like mergers and acquisitions, when due diligence is not performed, we can see a massive negative influence ripple (even if it doesn't happen for years). Issues like team culture, policies and procedures, employee retention, and more can begin to surface. By merging two companies with different cultures, everyone on the team might be confused and upset by the change, especially when communication is poor or inconsistent prior to the merger or acquisition. When individuals work for a team they love that suddenly changes, they may decide to leave. Not performing due diligence when making decisions in life and in business can cause negative effects that may not have been intended.

Each choice we face, whether personal or professional, has an influence on us and on those around us. Our influence is how we become the "I" in our teams. The best way to ensure that our decisions are the most positive influence on our teams is to magnify the process by slowing it down and performing due diligence. Slowing down allows us to question all aspects of each of the choices we may not understand or even know, and making decisions in an informed way is how we can all stay educated and positive. It's also how we can live with our decisions in the future.

If we know that we performed due diligence when making our decisions, we will have less regret in the future. We will second-guess ourselves less. Even if the decision we made turns out to be wrong, or not so great, we will still find peace in knowing that we elected an educated choice to the best of our ability. There is always chance (and often risk) in making decisions, no matter how much due diligence we perform. That's what makes them fun, maybe even a little scary. For example, if we make the life decision to go back to school or join a club or sport, we need to be sure we ask ourselves if we have the time, money, and commitment level to alter our lives by adding more to it.

When we make decisions, we are altering the future of our choices. This doesn't mean that whatever choice we didn't choose won't come up again—it just might come up in a different way. Decisions launch us into a new pool of choices, where we begin the cycle all over again. This can be from anything as small as choosing what to eat for breakfast to choosing to merge two companies. Our decisions have an impact on our life, no matter how small. Just as our influence has an impact in this life, no matter how small.

After we are faced with choices and we land upon a decision, we cannot remain stagnant by just deciding. Then we must follow through with action in order to reach the desired result of that decision. Acting means there will be change, hopefully for the better.

Change can be off-putting, but once you decide (or not decide), you act. To be a positively influential leader, you must follow your decisions with actions that lead you toward the goal of that decision.

Key Takeaways: Choice and Decision

- Decision and choice are quite similar, but choice comes before decision. Choice is theoretical, while decision is final and concrete.
- Only by knowing yourself fully and understanding who you want to be can you make the best decisions.
- Slow down to bring clarity to the decisions you make by performing due diligence (research). This removes the need to be impulsive and could curb second-guessing your decisions down the road.

Action and Inaction

Change is taking action. By taking action, we embark on a journey to produce change either within ourselves or others. As we explored in the previous section, sometimes change can be uncomfortable, meaning the actions to get us there can be uncomfortable, too. Some of us like to feel secure, or stagnant, in our positions in life, and can adapt to things that are inefficient, dangerous, or unhealthy. We may even fight to keep those negative situations stable. There is a certain fear in what the unknown holds for us, no matter how unremarkable the unknown may be in the grand scheme of things. We will protect the status quo despite ourselves, and it is this tendency that makes taking action so difficult.

I chose to title this section "Action and Inaction" because I think it's important to realize that even when we choose *not* to act upon something, we are still actively choosing. Just like *not* making a decision is a decision. Therefore, there is no true inaction. We are still deciding not to act. An example of this would be smoking. When we commit to stop smoking, we are committing to much more than no longer lighting a cigarette. We are choosing to alter our lives and the lives of those around us. By choosing inaction (not smoking) in this scenario, we positively influence ourselves, our financials, and our teams.

The decision to no longer smoke propels us into a realm that requires action. We will need to get rid of all our remaining cigarettes, clean all our clothes and spaces of cigarette smoke, and ensure that we remove the temptations from our lives so we refrain from smoking again. Action and inaction are intertwined in a dance between choosing and refraining. They are synced, meaning that we are never in a state of pure inaction.

The moment we begin affecting change across multiple people or within our organizations, action and inaction become even more complex. Most of my job involves change. From adaptation of a new idea, to updating company policies, to helping clients with succession planning and mergers and acquisitions, nearly my entire job revolves around supporting our clients to make changes to their companies for the better. Each of our clients is unique and requires an individualized approach to improving their companies in the long term; essentially, we are hired to affect change.

The process of change requires continuous switches, on and off, of action and inaction. Along the way, we may discover that processes or policies and procedures aren't working, which will then require change to make them work. Similarly with people: Even when people resist the change in our programs and think they are not participating, by resisting they are acting against the change. Meaning, the amount of effort to change is the same amount of effort to act against the change (inaction). People have various reasons for resisting change and action through inaction, and they may believe that the way things are is better than the way things could be.

The action of not acting is still influential and may be positive or negative, depending on the situation. Positive change requires participation; it cannot happen on its own. If you recognize that an action is having a positive influence on those around you, something as simple as recognizing that with your peers can have a dramatic outcome on that change. By embracing change, you can lead others to embrace it, too. This will not only make the process smoother as you work together, but the team can all move toward the same goal.

Through open communication with your team, you can make the change more stable and tolerable. By setting expectations and discussing the actions that will occur throughout the change process with everyone, you eliminate some of the fears that come with change. When everyone is on the same page about where you are heading, they will feel more inclined to act in unison. If you recognize that change can be uncomfortable, you can create an open space to discuss these feelings of discomfort.

Of course, there will be those who negatively challenge change and resist. These individuals can make the process of change and action more difficult for the rest of the team as they choose to embark on the journey of inaction. It's important to listen to the concerns of those who resist change. Their fears may be felt by others. As a positive leader, your team deserves to be listened to and have their fears addressed. This doesn't necessarily mean that they will decide to come aboard, but they will respect that you listened to them. Communicating openly may lessen their resistance. As the change slowly occurs, they may become more open to the possibility of acting, too.

We can be successful if we accept that success requires change. Success comes with many challenges, and we won't get anywhere in life by remaining passive. As we continue through life, and the change that comes with it, don't dismiss the random occurrences. Everything happens for a reason, and all actions contribute to balance. This is why listening and observing are so important, especially during proactive change. We must be in tune with the change and with those around us to ensure that we end up where the change was meant to take us.

Action also breeds responsibility. When we decide to take action that affects other individuals, and not just ourselves, we must remember that our influence is the single greatest responsibility we have as human beings. When we choose to take action, it is our responsibility to ensure that we pursue those actions to the best of our ability to minimize any negative impacts. For example, I discussed in a previous chapter how I changed our hiring policies and left it to my team to do the hiring without discussing my expectations with them. I chose to act (changing the policy and delegating hiring) but failed to ensure that the project was pursued correctly, which resulted in a negative impact. The same can be said about inaction: If you choose inaction, you must ensure that your choice not to act doesn't have a negative effect on your team.

Part of taking action, or even inaction, requires some willpower. There are times when we feel fed up with the results of our efforts or the efforts of others. The influence these feelings have can sap our willpower tank and lead us to inaction. We may feel defeated, burnt out, worn down, or simply over the situation at hand, leading us to give up. Once we choose a path, we mustn't give up. We owe it to ourselves to see it through and finish. Take a break to rebuild your willpower to push through.

One action we can all try to master is the act of building up our willpower. Have you ever been at work and just hit a wall? Making hard decisions, feeling stressed, or even just feeling drained can take a toll on your tank of willpower. I know, for me, there is a feeling I get when I am just done for the day; usually, I know that feeling is coming up before I even get there. If you can identify the times when you feel like you're about to hit a wall, try refilling your tank of willpower immediately. It may be difficult, and it's subjective. Once you can master this art, it will positively influence you for the rest of your life. One way you can refill your tank is by stepping away from whatever problem you are working on and taking a break. That could be switching to another task that is less taxing, taking a walk, chatting with a team member for a moment, getting some tea, turning the lights off and meditating for a few minutes, or anything you can think of that will bring you peace and back to center. Try different approaches and see what works best for you.

If you can set a good example for your team by showing them how you refill your willpower, you can positively influence them to avoid feeling burnt out. They may ask you what you're doing differently. If you can lead your team with the last drop of willpower you have, and even refill that willpower when it has seemingly run out, you can be the catalyst that positively influences them to keep going. On the other hand, if you fail to master your willpower and your team sees you give up, even before their tanks are empty, they may choose to follow your path and give up, too.

This doesn't mean that you always have to be the strongest one. We are all human, and we all have our bad days. If you are a positive influence and leader, even on your bad days, your team will be there to carry you through to the end. They will respect that you have done the same for them and will return that favor to you when you need it. That is why it is called teamwork.

Just as willpower can be contagious, inaction can be, too. If you can imagine a company with lazy leaders, you know that their subordinates and team will be lazy, too. People who aren't lazy won't tolerate working in an environment where they are the only one trying. Only lazy people will be attracted to lazy environments. This is not to say that inaction is always lazy. As we mentioned previously, inaction can result from the fear of change. It's important to keep an open mind and listen to your team when presented with inaction in order to realize the root cause.

Actions define us. Who we are and who we are perceived to be relies heavily upon the actions we take. We are not solely measured by the words we say, but by the actions we take in support of those words. For example, if we are part of a team and are consistently participating in a discussion about an action that is needed, but we fail to follow through on those opinions with action, we are creating a negative influence. Our ability to act upon our opinions and words creates our legacy. It's how the world perceives us. If we're all talk and no walk, people won't take what we say seriously.

Key Takeaways: Action and Inaction

- Even when you decide not to act, you are still actively choosing. Just as not making a decision is a decision, there is no true inaction because you are still deciding to not act.
- Choosing the route of inaction can often make action for others more difficult, especially if they rely on you.
- Action breeds responsibility. When you decide to take action that affects several other individuals, and not just yourself, you must remember that your influence is the single greatest responsibility you have.
- When you feel the effects of stress and burnout, consider how you might rebuild your tank of willpower to feel better. This could be anything from taking a walk, having a cup of tea, doing yoga, playing a video game, or whatever it is that makes you feel content and energized.

Change Reflection

The most influential thing we can do for ourselves and our teams is to get involved. Act and lead by example: A good leader takes action. We use the tools we have developed to analyze our choices, make decisions, and put into action what is needed to reach the outcome of our decisions. This requires continuous education, so we make more informed decisions, but it is worth it. When we view change as an opportunity to learn, we can make decisions and follow through with those decisions successfully.

CHAPTER 5
SELF-EDUCATION

> **"Education is the most powerful weapon which you can use to change the world."**
> **—Nelson Mandela**

We each live through experiences and challenges that are different from those of the other 8 billion people on this planet. Each day, we are also responsible for how these experiences educate us. This is where self-education begins. These lessons are springboards into further learning opportunities, but it is our choice to continue the self-education process.

Everything you have read thus far has been part of your self-education journey, which is a great thing because you need to educate yourself in order to be a positive influence. I believe that in order to be influenced *and* to be influential, you need to find your drive for that influence. Whatever your motivation was to read this book, you embarked on a journey of self-education. You may be learning new things, coming up with ideas on your own, or solidifying what you already know.

From my experience, humans like to learn. Maybe not all of us prefer to learn in a classroom or in a structured manner, but there is likely some part of us that enjoys the process of learning. We like and want our statements and actions to be accurate, which requires us to continue to learn. I've never met anyone who enjoyed making a mistake or an incorrect statement. We are constantly absorbing information, some better and faster than others. Obviously, there are things in life we cannot teach ourselves, which is why we seek out schooling, mentors, books, and more to educate us.

Some people view education as something that should or can only be accomplished through schooling or in a formal setting. They dismiss the lessons of life and chalk them up to something other than education. We see this a lot in the business world, where countless companies I have worked with are looking to hire someone with the "education" to get the job done. However, they discount experience. What is experience? It's applied education. When working with these companies, I can usually point out someone within their organization who already has the résumé for the job, minus the formal education.

I am not dismissing formal education; I am simply arguing that by dismissing education outside of the classroom, companies are excluding some of the smartest people available for the position. Not everyone has the opportunity to be formally educated, but that doesn't diminish their smarts or ability to learn rapidly. The world is our school, and every human on the planet is a student. We are all constantly receiving lessons in every setting.

Self-education, on its own, is influential, so you have the opportunity to influence yourself daily. Each time you maintain your composure, take the high road, hold yourself accountable, or act humbly, you are reinforcing or learning something new. Through this book, you may find a connection to a story or a concept, leading you to your own ah-ha moment where you get more clarity about yourself that reinforces prior learning and understanding. Training, or trying to make a habit, is another way of saying you are educating yourself to behave in a new way. Thus, the process of self-education is perpetual.

As we learn, we more fully understand the gravity of our responsibility—our influence. We learn from our failures and observe the new obstacles or opportunities they create for change and growth. We learn how to be consistent in our actions to create more balance in our lives. The more we learn about ourselves, the better influence we can be for others. When we know ourselves, we can open ourselves up to others; in that way, we can educate them about who we are. When we know others and others know us, we can approach situations with an understanding of one another.

One of the most important lessons I have had in life—at the risk of being a broken record—is slowing down. I cannot emphasize enough how important this is. The art of slowing down will take time, but without self-education, you will not be able to slow down consistently. Learning something new takes practice and application. Each time you apply the art of slowing down, you will reinforce what you learned. Also, as life continues to accelerate, partially due to the role of technology, slowing down will continue to challenge you and those around you; on the positive side, this creates a continuous opportunity to learn how slowing down benefits you. When you slow down, you can take advantage of your present opportunities through situational awareness. If you fail to slow down, life will attempt to balance you out.

We have infinitely more educational opportunities through our personal lives once we choose to slow down. These lessons are embedded in our everyday experiences when we get into the right frame of mind, beyond immediate gratification or the disappointment of the moment. Learning from our own experience means listening to (or actively observing) the experience of others, too. My observations about learning from others led me to write this series with stories in hopes that they can be good teaching lessons.

I cannot tell you how many times I have heard someone say, "Learn from my experience." We can learn infinite lessons from our interactions with others. When we open ourselves up to the perceptions of those around us, we become more educated, cultured, and aware. The people around us offer opportunities to learn from them. As such, the art of self-education can be as simple as listening, giving ourselves permission to learn, and having the willpower to overcome the urge to only learn our own lessons.

When we recognize our tendency to solely want to learn from our own lessons and ignore the lessons others have learned, we will be ready to make that leap. This itself is a learning opportunity. Sometimes it takes repetitive negative results or a negative path to provide us with a complete understanding of that lesson. Some of the most common lessons that could be better learned if we observed others are things like procrastination, dabbling in drugs, being impulsive with money, and gossiping or spreading rumors.

Self-accountability is the hardest part of learning from others. When we observe or learn about someone else's learned-from mistakes, we don't have the same perception of the consequences when compared to making our own mistakes. Even if we have a high EI (emotional intelligence) or high capacity for empathy, it can be difficult for us to fully weigh consequences that aren't our own, thus, making self-accountability and learning from others more difficult. Even if we want to learn from them, it might be that we can't grasp the lesson until we go through it ourselves.

One dramatic example, which I mentioned in the first book, is my own experience with drugs in high school. I dove into dealing drugs in high school, which I knew were bad and illegal, despite all the positive influence from the people around me. I had some issues with the law, but because I was a minor, the penalties were fewer. However, due to my ego, I took those lessons for granted. Two months after my 18th birthday, and prior to my high-school graduation, I was arrested as an adult. The result of this arrest was joining the Army because I was given the option to join the Army or go to jail. While joining the Army turned out well for me, it was a hard lesson to learn at the time, and I never turned back to drugs.

I believe it is human nature for us to prefer to learn things more intimately, through self-education. In the post-COVID world, self-education is becoming more prevalent, especially with independent education in the form of eLearning. Independent learning has been available for quite some time and used to be called correspondence courses before eLearning. However, post-pandemic, we are seeing one of the largest mobilizations of eLearning ever attempted. Through online learning tools, we can go at our own pace, or we may join a "teacher" and "classroom" for a selected period. However, the success of these educational platforms varies, sometimes due to quality of material and sometimes due to the effort we each put in.

Through my experience, I have noticed that those who choose to learn online often learn the subject matter better than those who sat through a formal schooling structure. The reason, I believe, is that they have better context for learning as the lessons apply to either something in their life currently or they are choosing to study something they have a deep interest in. Context is vitally important in the self-education process. I believe people generally don't learn from others' lessons because they don't have the context to make those lessons relatable. I also don't dismiss those who lack or have less formal (in the classroom) education than others because it is very possible that their life experiences make them more qualified.

In fact, those who have formal education may be lacking the willpower to learn, and those who don't have formal education may have plenty of willpower to learn. Ultimately, willpower helps us to achieve self-education in a more proactive way. But, like gas in a car, our willpower can run out. We only have a certain amount of willpower to spend on a daily, weekly, or monthly basis. We all need to recognize the indicators when our willpower is beginning to run out and how we can either stay committed or increase our willpower.

Slowing down and willpower are two pillars in the self-education process, but how do we use these tools to make the lessons we want to learn stick? Self-education can take repeated action and practice to sink in. However, once we learn something through practice, it becomes a part of who we are. It's like building muscle; we have to put in the reps. For example, learning a new language. It's one thing to learn a language in a classroom, book, or online course, but it's an entirely different thing to put that learning into real-world action. This is why the most common advice we come across while learning a new language is that we must "use it or lose it."

Another challenge of self-education is not knowing what type of learner you are. Knowing your learning style, or combination of learning styles, comes from observing yourself. The most common learning styles are visual, auditory, and kinesthetic; however, there are several more. You may have to do some research and learn through trial and error to figure out your style. It's important to know what type of learner you are in order to get the most out of any learning experience.

For those who are auditory learners, it may be better to listen to podcasts or audiobooks, sit down in a classroom for a lecture, or listen to others who share their experiences. For someone who is a visual learner, online classes may be a great tool. Finally, kinesthetic learners are tactile, meaning they want to physically be able to touch and move while they are learning; they may not learn as much while sitting still or being a non-active participant. Your ability to progress in self-education depends on how you learn and how you retain information best.

Next, it is up to you to decide what you want to learn. Learn about things that interest you, that you want to become better at, or learn simply for the sake of learning. While you are constantly learning through life experiences, you surely also want to enjoy life through hobbies and conversation. If there are conversations you want to have, but don't know much about the topic, self-educate; if there is a new hobby you want to pick up but don't know where to start, self-educate.

Your education is in your hands, and you are more than capable of finding tools to learn more. Our world has abundant opportunities available to learn about an infinite number of things. To be a positive influence on your teams, you must keep learning. However, you must be mindful of the pitfalls that await you on your journey toward self-education. While you are trying to educate yourself, distractions can prevent you from making progress and retaining knowledge.

Distraction

Distraction is one of the biggest challenges we face while learning. Life itself can be a distraction. For example, we can be a distraction to ourselves if we get swept away in the particulars of our day-to-day life or have our heads in the clouds daydreaming and lose touch with the world around us. There are several types of distractions that can have different influences on us, zapping our willpower to learn. My hope is that by discussing some of these distractions, we can learn how to use them to our advantage to influence our ability to self-educate and maintain our willpower.

The biggest distraction to self-education is defaulting to a state of comfortable focus, or autopilot, which we discussed in detail in *Individual Influence*. Comfortable focus is something we all find ourselves in daily. When we are so accustomed to something, like our daily commute, we become comfortable in those acts. Our minds wander off while we trust our muscle memory and relaxed focus to get us where we are going. Comfortable focus can be defined as two things: 1) when we are so hyper-focused on our lives that we are thinking too much and therefore become distracted from the real world; or 2) we are too tired to think at all and therefore begin running on a type of "autopilot" (like driving home, which also distracts us from the real world in our minds).

Comfortable focus distracts us from much of what is going on around us, and that distraction impedes our ability to self-educate. We can miss out on life's lessons when we aren't paying attention. The best way to correct comfortable focus is to slow down. Thankfully, by identifying a problem, we are halfway toward solving it. Yet falling into a comfortable focus isn't the only thing that can distract us from our ability to self-educate.

Technology is another area where we can become distracted. In part, technology can make us more efficient and give us an opportunity to acquire information more quickly. This can be true, but the habits we develop when using technology don't typically support this theory. For one, there is social media. Cell phones and social media have become some of the most prolific distractions we have. Never before have we had the tools to interrupt our lives and the lives of others so pervasively.

I have visited clients with cubicles of employees in rooms of 10, 20, and even more, and I have observed, by the minute, the distractions that social media offers. I have run experiments with clients where we track employees' website use, and almost without fail during these experiments, we have witnessed multiple people accessing social media multiple times per hour. In one of these studies, the client was losing 20 working hours per week due to employees accessing social media; meaning the staff spent 20 hours as a group per week on social media. Interestingly enough, another observation we have made during the COVID-19 pandemic is with our clients' teams working from home. We have had several clients tell us that their employees run out of work to do, even though their workloads are exactly the same. What's missing is the distractions created at work, like chatting with team members and checking social media. When people work from home, they want to be done sooner; on the other side, before working from home, they had to fill their 8:00 a.m. to 5:00 p.m. with something.

The internet has become more than just a place to communicate with friends. It's also where we acquire our news, go shopping, educate ourselves, and more. We are emotionally and psychologically addicted to digital media. It's one distraction that affects most humans today—not just at work, but in our daily lives. In terms of distractions, right behind digital media consumption is texting and using our smartphones. Though texting is embedded in social media with the use of direct messaging, the *act* of texting or messaging is the distraction.

Texting has become such a distraction that it has been outlawed while operating motor vehicles in most states. When we are engaged in a conversation, we may go from a comfortable focus into something much more dangerous: Blind focus. Blind focus is a type of distraction we may fall into when absolutely nothing around us can get our attention unless it physically challenges us. With blind focus, we may have selective hearing and legitimate tunnel vision where our peripherals go black.

Have you ever witnessed someone walking along—head down, texting, scrolling, what have you—and right before they run into someone, or a wall, they are jarred out of their blind focus? You only need to observe people on the street to experience this type of distraction first-hand. I find it comical that these same people, who are so absorbed in their phones, treat the act of walking into someone or something as the distraction. As if running into someone or something was the annoyance, and not being nose-deep in their phone, ignoring the world around them!

One of the saddest stories I have about blind focus is from a peer of mine; he is the president of a small franchise company in the United States. He was visiting one of the franchisee worksites and was standing on the ground with the owner of the franchise. Above them, there were some workers on the roof. One of the workers was texting with someone with whom he had a deep emotional attachment; during that time, he walked off the roof. He didn't even look up from his phone as he stepped off the roof. Sadly, he lost his life. This is why blind focus is dangerous.

Are there any good distractions, or are they all bad? Some may argue that the information they learn from the communication in their texts is worth the distraction. Or that people should learn from the experiences of running into people or almost driving off the road—but do they? Distractions are negative when they interrupt our ability to be a positive influence. That means that any distraction that impedes our ability to do what is right and does not contribute to us doing good is negative.

Divided Attention

Multitasking is another form of distraction. When we attempt to do more than one thing at a time, we are distracted, which takes time away from each thing we are attempting to perform. I firmly believe that multitasking takes away from the value of what we are doing. One common example of multitasking is reading and watching TV. We can't focus 100 percent on what we are reading if we are also trying to focus on what is playing on TV. If you don't believe me, try reading a new book and watching a new show—one that is at least 30 minutes. Have someone give you a test on what you have read and watched, and there is a high percentage you won't even come close to acing both.

There are some people who have an uncanny ability to divide their focus, but these people are exceptions. Unfortunately, the rest of us use them as examples and fool ourselves into thinking we are multitaskers, too. We may be multitaskers, but at a high cost of quality to the individual tasks. By trying to divide our minds between two or more separate tasks, we diminish our ability to think clearly about just one of those tasks. When we distract ourselves, it can take our minds anywhere from 10 to 15 minutes to get back on track; multitasking divides our minds several times per minute, never allowing it to fully catch up.

For example, if you're working on tasks for one client and you allow another client to distract you, you cease performing the work of the first in favor of the second. If you attempt to handle both issues at the same time, the distraction of multitasking will reduce the effectiveness of your attention to one or both of your clients. You're not giving either of them your best or 100 percent of your attention. Furthermore, the chance of making a mistake increases, and your effectiveness and productivity decrease overall.

There are simple ways to deal with client-centric distractions. The first is setting proper expectations and boundaries for your clients. When you set proper expectations, you relieve yourself of the pressure to answer their requests and communications immediately. You can also let them know that you have received their request and that it has been queued to be addressed by the next available person in your organization. Setting the correct parameters with all clients by establishing their expectations is critical to minimizing distractions. You can also do the same with co-workers, so you can work without interruptions or distractions.

There are always exceptions, like the client who doesn't understand or accept that they have to wait. I have found that these people are usually living in a distracted environment, so they expect everyone around them to behave in the same distracted way. Either that or they think they deserve more attention than your other clients. Open communication with difficult clients about why distractions detract from your ability to perform may help them understand. After all, they wouldn't want you to be distracted while you were working with them.

In addition, distraction is a byproduct of micromanaging. By micromanaging, you disrupt the efficient workflow and thoughtflow processes of others. If you develop a hierarchy and then ignore that hierarchy because you feel your input or knowledge is required for every path in the decision-making process, then you are distracting from the intended advantages of others giving their input. Micromanagement is typically seen in organizations without structure.

With a lack of structure comes a lack of trust that the people can fulfill the goals or missions of the organization. By developing proper structure within an organization—including the ability to trust subordinates, peers, and leaders—you can develop an environment where learning is enabled and self-education can be fulfilled. On the other hand, by micromanaging, you interrupt that person's opportunity to learn and the team's opportunity to learn the capabilities that person has to handle whatever task is given to them.

Distractions affect us by impeding the full impact of influence we should be receiving or giving. Each time we are distracted, there is a cost. That cost varies based on what we are being distracted from. There can also be unintended consequences of distractions that can have a negative influence on us. For example, if I'm working on a project, learning a lot and focused on the subject matter, a distraction may cause me to lose context or a train of thought that could have been helpful. Depending on the task, this could be dire. Sometimes being on the right train of thought is all you need to turn something from an okay project into a great project.

We've discussed some of the worst-case scenarios of how distractions can affect us, such as accidents that can cause harm to property and life, but there are other negative outcomes that are not so dire. Distractions can be detrimental to relationships and cause issues between peers, subordinates, friends, and family. With cell phones, email, social networking, open work environments, and more, distractions are everywhere. Some of us have careers that are full of opportunities for distractions; we may always need to be available, not providing us an opportunity to limit our distractions.

However, there is hope. There are some good ways we can manage distractions, at least to the point where we manage our actions during times when we can't control outside distractions. This means limiting the number of tasks we work on during periods when we may become most distracted and using our calendar to block off time for deep or creative work. We also need to communicate to others that a closed door or a note at our workstation indicates "Do not disturb." Separating ourselves is one of the best ways to increase our concentration. This doesn't mean we stop work altogether; it just means we select tasks that allow for distraction when we know we are going to be distracted. Tasks that require deeper thought are then reserved for when we are less likely to be distracted.

Another way to minimize distractions is to change the way our email, phone, or social media delivers notifications. People are often reluctant to limit their phone access because our phones are the main way family can get in contact with us in the event of an emergency. But there is a super cool feature on phones where we can set specific contacts to still ring, even when our phone is on Do Not Disturb; it's called "favorites." In addition, we can turn off or close our email when we need to focus on a project or task. These strategies work for people who have the discipline to limit their communications at work; however, so much communication is done out of habit and not emergency. It's borderline an abuse of time.

If we can better manage the distractions in our life, we will have better retention and results. Our ability to self-educate will increase as we pay more attention to the world around us. We can maintain more focused concentration on our tasks, have better situational awareness, and learn more about the process we are in and the path we are taking to complete the tasks. Our self-education will be positively affected by a reduction in distractions, and we can increase our positive influence.

Finally, delays are another byproduct of distraction—like procrastination. Procrastinators often make the excuse that they are distracted, so they need to put more pressure on themselves to complete tasks. To be a positive influence, we need to understand that sometimes *we* are the distraction. By forcing ourselves into procrastination, we aren't setting ourselves up for success. Procrastination impedes our ability to self-educate.

Key Takeaways: Distraction

- Distractions are negative when they interrupt your ability to be a positive influence. Any distraction that impedes your ability to do what is right, and does not contribute to doing good, is negative.
- You can become a distraction to yourself if your day grows long, you lose time daydreaming, or you otherwise begin to lose touch with the world. This is often propelled by comfortable focus, which is when you become hyper-focused and begin to autopilot your thoughts and actions.
- Technology can be a distraction. While it can make you more efficient at times, some technology can hinder your productivity.
- Multitasking is another form of distraction. When you attempt to do more than one thing at a time, you are distracted, and this takes time away from each thing you are attempting to perform.
- Set boundaries to help yourself avoid distractions. For example, remove your phone from your work area, or consider changing the way your phone delivers notifications.
- Micromanaging causes distraction. Trust the person you delegated that task to and remove yourself as a distraction.
- You can avoid some of the issues of distraction by limiting the number of tasks you work on during periods when you may become most distracted; you can utilize your calendar to block off times for deep or creative work.
- You may try separating yourself from others if you find that they are distracting you. This could mean shutting your door,

putting your messages on Do Not Disturb, or letting others know you need time to focus.

Procrastination

I tend to be a procrastinator. I put off work because I have fooled myself into believing that, by procrastinating, I can put enough pressure on myself to increase my focus and decrease distractions. Procrastination may help in terms of adding pressure to get certain tasks done, but to truly be a positive influence on your team, you must learn not to procrastinate your tasks. Procrastination is a result of certain types of distractions (like having to let the dogs outside) and can also be the byproduct of continuous distractions (like getting lost in playing video games).

Having structure in place is one of the best ways to avoid procrastinating. A common theme in our series, if you have noticed, is structure—from developing structures within our company to helping our clients understand and build structure to support their organizational goals. If we don't have these structures in place, it eventually creates distractions and chaos. Without structure, team members all do their own thing, thinking they know the best way to go about it. When the team is not all on the same page, we are setting everybody up for failure. This goes for internal processes as well as external processes. Remember earlier when we were discussing consistencies between franchises and having the same experience with a company even in different locations? That is because of the structures they have in place to keep everything similar.

While procrastination can spur *some* people to meet goals and deadlines, there are unintended consequences of procrastination if other team members are involved. For example, it can have a negative effect on other team members as they wait for you to finish your work prior to proceeding with theirs. Procrastinating can be selfish because it can create risks for others. Procrastination can result in negative emotions amongst the team, such as anxiety or frustration. When dealing with procrastinators, we are generally dealing with distractors.

For example, say you're working on a project that takes advanced preparation. If you complete your tasks for the project early, you may have extra time to allot to other projects. If you have a colleague who has procrastinated and requires your assistance due to their procrastination, you now have a choice to make: Disrupt your current workflow to help them or ignore their request and run the risk of their procrastination disrupting the whole project. Either way, it becomes a distraction to you.

Procrastinators may live their lives in a perpetual state of procrastination simply because they don't know any other way. They may have a lack of organizational skills because they don't know how to structure their lives. Teams with these kinds of people will eventually break down because procrastination creates an influence ripple throughout the lives of more than just the procrastinator. There can be damage in the wake of procrastination that, over time, will eventually detract from any positive influence on the result. The stress involved for others when dealing with a procrastinator is itself a distraction. A negative work environment distracts people from being their best and is often reflected in their individual work product. When those who prepare in a more structured manner get ahead of those who procrastinate, the ability to work together is lost.

If you have someone like this on your team, try to help them learn how to organize and structure their days so they can develop habits for the betterment of the team. One of the best ways to reduce procrastination and become proactive is through time-blocking. Time-blocking is just what it seems: You block off time on your schedule to work on a designated task. By organizing your time in blocks and working on that designated task during that time, you can begin to set yourself up for success. Structure can solve a perpetual procrastinator's issues.

One of the best tools to influence your team is to apply your organizational skills. Being organized can alleviate distractions, procrastination, and chaos. Individuals who have completed formal education likely have been required to develop structure and organizational skills as part of the skillset or degree they obtained. The process of formal education involves a commitment to engaging with structure in order to complete your studies; even self-paced learning environments, like eLearning, have structure embedded in them to support independent learning while maintaining the organization needed.

Procrastination can also be an unintentional byproduct of an action like micromanaging. When we micromanage our team but express a commitment to delegating and allowing them to grow, we procrastinate their education. When we commit to giving authority to someone and then we take that away by distracting their efforts and micromanaging them, we are delaying or eliminating the opportunity for them to be a leader, have a positive influence, and learn. We also take away from our opportunity to learn about that person's capabilities.

This type of unintentional procrastination sets an organization up to have many distractions and challenges. If the goal is for the organization to be self-sufficient without direct continuous authority—by relying on the structure of process, procedure, and the experience of our subordinates—we may unknowingly procrastinate accomplishing that goal by micromanaging.

A good example of delaying progress through micromanaging can be seen during succession planning. We support several companies with succession planning at our company. The objective of this work is to transfer a leadership role to another individual in a structured way that satisfies the current leader. Their goal is to successfully transfer the influence of their position to a new individual. Many organizations don't have any structure or have very little, and it is limited to the owner/leader/manager maintaining control over most aspects of the operation.

A common issue we face during our succession planning happens after the leader agrees to change and engage with the program.

We may go a day, week, or month without issues, but as soon as there is a challenge where there is some discomfort, we will experience an obstacle. The leader may hear about the issue and immediately decide—because they are "still the boss"—to insert themselves into the process. Other times, an employee may need to engage with the "boss," but they choose to engage with the old boss and not the new one. These issues cause unintentional procrastination in the change management from the old boss to the new one and can cause a delay in the succession plan.

When we procrastinate out of a need to feel comfortable or to oppose change, it hurts more than just ourselves. Change is necessary for any viable, growing organization, and that includes when people need to move on to a new chapter in their life. Procrastinating does nothing more than put off negative feelings for one, two, or however many days. In fact, usually the negative feelings increase the longer the event or task is put off. The longer we wait to do something we know we need to do, the more our feelings of anxiety about doing that thing will grow.

Procrastination can only hold us for so long. There will come a point where we have to complete the task or event, and the act of procrastinating can make us rush through that task or event, leaving us to miss important details because we haven't left enough time. Rushing through anything isn't the best strategy, especially when we tie negative emotions to it. The longer we procrastinate, the faster we will have to work to get something done, and the higher the amount of risk we take for losing details that matter.

Key Takeaways: Procrastination

- Having structure and organization are two of the best ways to avoid procrastination. A lack of structure and organization can create distractions and chaos.
- Procrastination can be very selfish. While it may help add pressure to meet goals and deadlines, there are unintended

consequences if other team members are involved. When you procrastinate, you create risks for others.

- One of the best ways to reduce procrastination and become proactive is through time-blocking. Time-blocking is just like it sounds: It's when you block off time on your schedule to work on a designated task.
- Procrastination can be counterproductive if your intent is to do well but you ultimately need to speed up to catch up. Speed can sacrifice quality.

Attention to Detail

You may have people in your life who say to you, "Spare me the details, just get to the point." Generally speaking, though, the point *is* in the details. Details matter: "Make sure your 'I's are dotted and 'T's are crossed!" Paying attention to details doesn't need to be cumbersome. However, those who lack patience for the time it takes to absorb information may find it as such. Tell a story without details and context and you have a story that is flat, bland, and incomplete. Similarly, any task we set our minds to requires attention to detail in order for us to be accurate and successful.

When people put busyness ahead of accuracy in a leadership position, chaos almost always ensues. When accuracy is forgotten, the time required to fix issues that arise usually amounts to two or three times the time it would have taken to do it right in the first place. The people who do this try to work off memory, don't have a task or checklist, and usually just wing everything they do while boasting of their ability to multitask.

My team is always amazed when a report does not include details. If you miss details, gaps grow from day to day, week to week. People will begin to get used to operating with less detail and then want to avoid accountability when things begin to unravel, blaming the issues on not having the proper details. How often have you heard, "I didn't have all the information" as an excuse or reason for a poor outcome?

Part of your positive influence in a leadership position includes your responsibility to ensure that details and context are not missed. Leaders who don't ensure attention to detail can create unintended consequences and put their leadership influence in jeopardy. The bigger issue today is delivering details alongside a timeframe of expected results. This can be managed by: Planning efficiently, paying attention to details, ensuring time allotted is time needed, and setting goals to move forward.

Context is where details matter greatly. It is possible to hear or read facts and make wrong decisions based on those facts. Every industry has a way of putting their best image forward. Image is not always created from the details, and it is not always based on reality. One of the biggest places we see this abuse of image is through context and perception related to details in numbers. You can easily influence people's perception of context by using percentages without providing the details, which can spread negative influence through disinformation.

I have worked with several organizations with middle management that justified decisions or plans based on percentages with no context, causing near-catastrophic issues. Percentages can be one of the most misleading analytical tools accepted without including the details and context in which they were created. To give you an example of this, I would like to explore how percentages can create false perceptions (images).

Let's look at how sales growth can appear—for example, an 11 percent growth in sales. This identifies that revenue went up, but what about cost? How did margins perform? When our clients use single percentages to glorify something, we always follow up with questions to dig deeper. We have a client who added a type of machinery to their offerings. The average sale price of this product was $35,000, and the company was valued at $1.3 million. The company sold 4 sets of this machinery in the first year, increasing their revenue by 11 percent.

On the surface, the percentages might make it look like the company did well. However, the reality was that they were underwater regarding cash, and it would take either a big increase in sales of this new product or a few years to break even. The first year, their net profit dropped from $173,000 (their net profit average) to under $100,000 due to the distractions and costs involved with selling this new piece of equipment. The second year, profits went up to about $135,000, still far below the previous average of $173,000.

Unfortunately, skewing the analytics to show favorable percentages is common in business, and most people don't ask questions or dig deeper into what those percentages mean or where they came from. Another huge violator is in social media marketing metrics that present analytics without analyzing them first, which puts them out of context. If you were running a marketing campaign via Facebook, what would the most important metric be? I have asked several of my clients this question and they have responded with either "I don't know" or "likes."

What is a "like" to your business? How does that "like" translate to a return on investment (ROI)? How does that "like" define the relationship with that person? Typically, the next metric identified is "follow." How does someone following your social pages contribute to your company goal of selling products or services? For example, if your business needs to grow followers because it is an information company that uses the page to deliver information, those details put into context how a "follower" might be a valuable metric in your marketing campaign. However, if you're a widget sales company and someone follows you, what does that accomplish?

Let's assume your original goal is to grow your pages' likes/followers so that you have a base to market to. The posts are calls-to-action, click-throughs, visits, or calls. How are you getting these details? The purpose of any marketing campaign is to help you define the relationship. If you have 1,000 likes/followers and those followers don't engage with your content in any way, what value do those likes/followers have?

I'm sure you have heard the phrase "Peel the onion." Leaders should keep asking questions about the metrics or any information they receive that lacks in detail: Peel the onion. Ask where the data is coming from, how it was obtained, and for what purpose. When presented with percentages, dig deeper to find the details. When presented with summaries, get clarification on how the summary was prepared. Ensure that the content and context match.

One of our most recent client challenges involved a decline in sales on Amazon. While our client was in the middle of changing management, their Amazon sales declined. The owner felt inclined to immediately blame the change in management without looking into any further details. We convinced them to allow us to put together an analytical report of the history of sales and research the overall market as a comparison.

We learned that there was an immediate decline in sales after the change of management, lasting between two and three weeks. We then saw an increase in sales proportional to the effort put back into the transactional support for marketing once the new management was instated. In studying the market, we saw a broader decline. While sales rebounded from the change of management, they adjusted and continued to decline across the board. When comparing this data with their competitors' sales data, we identified a reduction of sales across the entire market segment that was akin to our client's decline—meaning the decline was primarily market-driven.

Finding the true culprit behind successes, declines, rises, or anything else is how we can determine how to move forward in the best way. If we attempt to move our goals forward without knowing the true context and details of where we are moving to, we could end up causing more damage to our business. Details about our client's context allowed us to prepare a strategy to disrupt the market conditions affecting our client's sales. Peel the onion and keep asking who, what, where, when, why, and how.

Having the proper details and paying attention to them is where positive influence stems from. When we make decisions or take actions without a proper understanding of the details or context, there is a high risk of us having a negative influence on ourselves or our teams. We need to challenge ourselves and our teams to understand the details and/or context of the issue prior to moving forward with decisions or actions.

One might ask why people fall for the trap of summation and accept it as the truth or as enough to act. My answer to that question would be intellectual laziness. We tend to get into the habit of accepting things that are delivered regularly. News is delivered the same way, every day, so we get in the habit of accepting it. We get this "comfortable focus" of what we believe in (confirmation bias). We all know a person who solely listens to FOX News or CNN; I'm sure many of you reading this are thinking negative thoughts about one or the other. I'm not here to defend any media outlets; what was once news is now opinion, and that is the point here. Regardless of where our information comes from, we tend to get very comfortable with our sources and take for granted (or assume) they are correct. We trust certain friends and family because they are smart. We trust social media, or parts of it, and share things with the click of a button, only to find out they were not true. Yes, respectable people can become complacent and lazy when it comes to receiving certain types of information.

One of the hardest things to do in our society is to differentiate between information that is correct and misinformation. With access to free self-education platforms—blogs, podcasts, articles, news, YouTube, and more—comes a risk of educating ourselves with the wrong information. During our self-education process, paying attention to the details is important, but so is keeping an open mind and not making assumptions. Don't take everything you read or hear at face value. Check sources and opposing information to try to get all the details possible regarding that subject.

When you are working on a team, you need to peel the onion. During your personal self-education process, you need to ask questions about the information you take in. If your goal is to become better at something, don't do it the wrong way. Find multiple sources for the information you wish to learn and figure out where the information remains consistent. Ask questions about information that is inconsistent. Keep asking questions until you conclude that it is well thought out and doesn't pose more questions.

When we become intellectually lazy, we cease to have the ability to learn new information. We become trapped in a cycle of our own confirmation bias and don't question ourselves. When we stop asking questions, we stop learning. Our goal in life should be to be our best selves and to have the best influence we can; that only comes from learning. Seize the moment and be intellectually aware.

Key Takeaways: Attention to Detail

- When you put busyness ahead of accuracy, chaos almost always ensues. The amount of time required to fix issues that arise as a result of foregoing accuracy usually amounts to two or three times the amount of work it would have taken to do it right in the first place.
- When you're a leader, it is your responsibility to ensure details and context are not missed. Leaders who don't ensure this can create unintended consequences and put their influence in jeopardy.
- You should ask questions about the information you receive that is lacking in detail: Peel the onion. Ask where the data is coming from, how it was obtained, and for what purpose. When presented with percentages, dig deeper to find the details. When presented with summaries, get clarification on how the summary was prepared.

Intellectual Laziness

Have you ever noticed that ex-smokers dislike current smokers the most? I am an ex-smoker, so being around a smoker can be very offensive. In my opinion, intellectual laziness is just like that. When we develop a habit of questioning data to the point that we seek details and context in almost every aspect of our lives, incomplete data spouted by intellectually lazy people can become amazingly offensive.

Not all those who supply incomplete data are intellectually lazy; some are just ignorant to the value that details and context have for positive influence. There are, however, many people who are intellectually lazy; they know that what they hear or see is not being delivered in proper context or with all the details, but they choose to do nothing about it because they feel that looking up the details is too much effort. These people are dangerous, and there are way too many of them in the world. They perpetuate the negative influence of others and reinforce it by passing on information to their peers, who are also intellectually lazy. Social media exacerbates this.

Intellectual laziness may be one of the most detrimental aspects humans face today. We are becoming increasingly more accepting of false or skewed information, believing that it is true without so much as a cursory challenge to the legitimacy of the content. We accept what we hear from politicians as true; however, if we ask any of our friends or family if they think politicians tell the truth, they will most likely say no.[5] How is it that we understand that politicians lie, yet we believe what they say to the point that we share that information and spread the lies? Intellectual laziness.

The phenomenon of disinformation is not limited to politics, but it is where I think we can see the biggest impact that intellectual laziness has on us as leaders and positive influencers. If we belong to

5. Healy, Melissa. "Voters Have High Tolerance for Politicians Who Lie, Even Those Caught Doing It." *Los Angeles Times*, 26 Dec. 2018, www.latimes.com/science/sciencenow/la-sci-sn-fact-checking-politicians-20181218-story.html

a group of intellectually lazy people, we may begin to recognize that people (including us) take advantage of that laziness. We once had a client who accepted mediocrity from their employees. They took for granted the amount of money they were making and became reckless in their collection and reporting of data. This issue resulted in our client not having detailed costing information until months after the work was complete.

One day, they asked us to review a package of data that identified that the company was losing money—tons of money—on a regular basis. This client, who had been a seven-figure earner, was now losing mid-six-figures halfway through the year. However, after five years of high six- and low seven-figure earnings, the client had not noticed these losses. Digging a bit further into the details, we identified a loophole in their policies and procedures where management could make on-the-fly decisions to use resources that, on the surface, were lucrative.

Middle management sold upper management on a program that utilized outsourced labor instead of in-house labor to complete work on jobs. For example, a laborer who was costing the company $100 per hour internally would now only cost $75 per hour. The team involved had 10 individuals, so the savings to the company was $250 per hour or $10,000 a week. The manager who put this program together had been with the company for a long time, and their projects were generally successful.

Next, middle management assembled a new program to buy certain products through a new supplier relationship. The manager told our client that they would receive a 10 percent discount with this new supplier. However, the devil was in the details. The middle manager actually owned the labor company and was an investor in the new supplier's company. Therefore, he was making $25 per hour for each laborer his company provided; so, while he was supposedly saving his employer $10,000 a week, he was simultaneously making $10,000 a week. Additionally, with the discount he got through the new supplier, he had negotiated a 30 percent discount but was turning around and giving his employer only 10 percent off.

The losses our client experienced were a direct result of these actions. Yes, he reduced the per-hour cost of labor by $25 and reduced the product cost for certain items by 10 percent. However, in doing so, he eliminated his accountability for job performance (which is how our client pays employees). As he became more comfortable with the amount of money he was making on the side, which was literally hundreds of thousands of dollars, he lost sight of his project management, and the jobs began losing money. A lot of these losses went directly into the middle manager's pocket; because the projects were taking longer, more was being spent in labor and supplies, so he made more on the side and our client lost more upfront. How did this happen? Intellectual laziness. Nobody involved in the decision-making process about the outsourced labor company or new supplier ever thought to question the legitimacy of why it was beneficial to make these changes. Essentially, the middle manager made themselves the "middleman" in every transaction between our client and their companies.

When this all came to light, we were faced with a huge leadership moment. The anger felt by everyone involved, except the middle manager making all the money, was intense. Of course, it can be easy to fire people or make decisions when emotions get the best of us. But this was a chance to resolve long-standing issues our client had faced for several years. Slowing down and calming the heightened emotions created an opportunity for the leading minds to come together to solve the issue with middle management and the issues that allowed them to get there.

I am aware that there is a lot going on in this particular example: Lack of structure, intellectual laziness, greed, ignorance, disrespect, failure to take responsibility for influence, and more. Still, it boils down to the fact that this middle manager was taking advantage of an already-flawed system created by ownership or upper management. The middle manager was afforded the opportunity to keep his job, with some added policies and procedures to ensure that conflicts of interest no longer occurred.

When we identify intellectual laziness in organizations, we follow the same procedure as we do when we are looking to gain more details: Peel the onion. How deeply has the laziness penetrated an organization? If an organization has an intellectually lazy leader, there are surely others who are lazy in the lower hierarchy of the organization. Some may think that having their head in the sand and trying to pretend that issues are not happening—or worse, accepting a bad situation because we don't like the conflict or challenge it presents—is a positive move, but it is not.

An organization's decision-making process reflects the culture in that organization. How individuals approach their work alone and with each other, and how they fulfill that work, is how culture is ultimately measured within an organization; it's how the team works, operates, and moves together. Take Google, for example, or another organization that has an open campus set up like a college campus. These organizations have amazing communication between peers, customers, and vendors. What we won't find in these organizations is a lot of intellectually lazy people.

Intellectually lazy leaders don't communicate well. They are always trying to find a way to delegate difficult decisions. If they are faced with a decision that they deem difficult, it is generally filled with emotion and a lack of detail, understanding, or empathy toward the issue that created the problem in the first place. Intellectual laziness creates a negative environment that, over time, places a high risk of failure on the overall organization, especially on the team. This is usually the case in organizations affected continuously by high employee turnover.

Another byproduct of intellectual laziness is impulsiveness. When someone is intellectually lazy, they tend to make impulsive decisions that lack thoughtful details. Intellectually lazy people will try to hide behind statements like "I'm the boss," "It's my risk to take," or other condescending remarks made to someone who may challenge their impulsive decision. Leaders like this can be very difficult. These types of leaders often exhibit this type of behavior in their personal lives, too.

If you have either self-identified or been called out as an intellectually lazy leader, the transition to thoughtful leadership will be challenging. Trust me, because I still struggle with being intellectually lazy sometimes. I have put my company at risk by being intellectually lazy, and more than once. From taking shortcuts in hiring employees to not following our own due diligence when we take on a project or buy a company, every time I make a mistake, I can identify a moment of intellectual laziness. From one leader to another, my best advice is to never make a major decision for your organization without allowing someone who is not a "yes person" to review the details of that decision. You don't have to follow that person's review or advice, but you should listen to them.

I have hastily hired people who, on the surface, appeared to be a good fit for our company based on two short interviews. I thought I liked them. Allowing someone to come into your organization should take more than just a cursory review of their résumé and meeting with them for 15 minutes to an hour. Be thoughtful about your hiring and the people you will trust to have an influence on the culture of your organization. Being thoughtful will help you go from being intellectually lazy to intellectually aware.

Becoming intellectually aware requires effort on our part through self-education, which can come in many forms, including life experience. We don't always have to be learning from something or someone. Sometimes our opportunities to grow come from ourselves, by the way we choose to live our lives. When we choose to live in a positive way and lead with a positive influence, those lessons will also be positive. How we choose to view even the negative occurrences in our life will influence our ability to learn.

Key Takeaways: Intellectual Laziness

- Intellectual laziness is when you know that the information being delivered to you is false or missing context and you choose to do nothing about it.
- If you find that you are acting impulsively, ask if it's due to intellectual laziness. Impulsive actions are usually made in haste, which means research can suffer and laziness can govern decision-making.
- You should never make a major decision for your organization without allowing someone who is not a "yes person" to review the details of that decision.

Self-Education Reflection

Don't underestimate yourself. Leaders who choose to remain intellectually active by staying engaged in their decision-making and actions understand the value they bring as an individual to the teams they influence. They understand that by remaining inactive or lazy, they don't contribute their best self to their team. Who you are and how you choose to continuously develop yourself elevates the teams around you. The more of yourself you can offer—meaning the more you know yourself and develop your unique influence—the more you can contribute to the cultures that surround you. After all, cultures are built by people's influence. Choose to be a leader who strives to continuously add positivity to the cultures you belong to.

Chapter 6
Diversity, Equity, and Inclusion

> **"The beauty of the world lies in the diversity of its people."**
> **—Unknown**

Often, we can be tricked by our ego and/or bias into treating people as objects and seeing ourselves as residing above them in an almost authoritarian way. This chapter is primarily about viewing people as people and doing our best to treat them as such. With such an important topic, one that has the potential to deeply impact the places where people come together (home, school, work, etc.) and our ability to be a positive influence, our goal is to remain as objective as possible while highlighting multiple positions to demonstrate the beauty of diversity and perspective. Through this goal, we do not wish to segregate, isolate, or perpetuate more hate within our society; we believe that bigotry in any form is negative. If we look at society closely, our aims to create spaces of equality often lead to bigotry being used as a tactic to alleviate bigotry (and it fails). We do not wish to add to this discussion; rather, we aim to spark a discussion around the true meaning of diversity.

What is True Diversity?

You may wonder why this section refers to "true" diversity rather than simply "diversity." In our more mainstream conversations, we tend to limit our discussions of diversity to the topics of race, gender, and sexual orientation; however, while these three things can define diversity, it is truly so much more. If we are going to continue to inspire discussions of diversity with our teams, we believe we must include a wider variety of differences that continue to push the boundaries of diversity.

While this list may seem to run long, we are simply trying to document all the areas of diversity we see. And while this is certainly not an exhaustive list and you may think of more points to add, one of our goals is actually to influence you to become an influencer of positive diversity. We want to engage you in thinking about how people are diverse in more ways than the ones we mention here. After this paragraph, you will find an image with a representation of an iceberg, demonstrating the things we can see and cannot see within a person. The top of the iceberg and traits mentioned here are some things that we might be able to see when meeting each other, and the items below the iceberg are things that make us even more diverse but which we cannot see. The deeper we go, the more intimate information we can discover. Do any of these resonate with you?

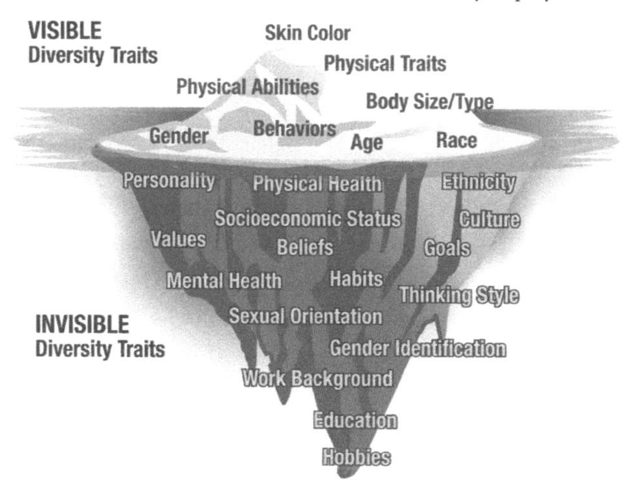

Diversity includes both how we are alike *and* how we are different. While nobody on this earth is exactly like us as individuals, we may bond with those who have similar traits, whether or not they are defined by visible or invisible characteristics. However, while we may resonate more with those who are like us, if we become too caught up in this way of thinking, it can lead us to perpetuate a culture of "us versus them," which instigates negativity, bias, and bigotry. This is a denial and an inability to accept those who are dissimilar to you. But why do we do this? Why do we buy into the notion that we must dismiss, hate, or shame others and create turmoil for ourselves and them in the process?

Since birth, many of us have been fed a mantra that in order to survive and be successful, we must get ahead of others by always being in motion and doing more; this is often portrayed as oppression, bias, bigotry, and other negative actions. We incorrectly believe that this is the only way we can create space for ourselves and feel accepted or part of something we resonate with. It's almost as if we believe there is limited space in the world for love and success, so if we knock others down to climb upwards, then we are saving ourselves. In truth, we are hurting ourselves *and* others with our negative influence. It should be painfully obvious that when we create a world where it is culturally acceptable to segregate based on any kind of diversity, we hurt all of humanity.

One of the challenges we face is the commingling of culture and diversity, which don't always go hand in hand. There are times when issues can be identified as stemming from culture, such as racism. In the late 1990s and early 2000s, I was traveling for a client and often found myself in South Carolina. While out grocery shopping one day, I opened the door for an elderly Black woman. She stopped and verbally refused to walk through. Confused and curious as to why, I asked her. She stated that she would not be looked on well for allowing a White man to hold the door for her; she seemed somewhat peeved and surprised at my curiosity and did not understand why I was inquiring. But then she shared, more quietly, that she didn't have any issues with interactions like this because it's just how it was and how it had always been in her life.

How do we live in a country where freedom is valued but racism is baked into the very culture of parts of our nation? Unfortunately, this is not solely an American issue; it's a human issue.

Another example I have regarding racism comes from across the pond around the same time I had this experience in South Carolina. I was attending an international association meeting and noticed, upon arrival, that there were no women or people of color (and this was not an accident). One might be able to dismiss something like this, but I made easy note of it. When the conversation started, I realized why this was not an accident; every person in attendance was openly antisemitic (prejudiced toward Jews). Since my last name is Smith, the people in the room felt comfortable being openly antisemitic around me, stating that this was because "it's obvious you aren't Jewish with a name like Brian Smith." (In fact, my mother's maiden name is Goldstein, and we have Jewish heritage.)

Examples like these help us understand what was stated earlier; there is something within humans that makes us believe we must perpetuate an "us versus them" mentality, which then becomes our culture. For those that are oppressed, it can't be questioned; for the oppressor, bigotry thrives. It's impossible to know what people are like or who they are just by simply looking at them or knowing their last name. Even after having a conversation, there is so much below the surface that we may never know. For example, while someone may look White, we may end up discovering that they have a multi-faceted family history that includes recent immigration or a religious or ethnic identity we didn't anticipate.

It's easy to look at people and apply our bias to them, but what good does that do? How does this bias harm us and our cultures? In the situations mentioned above, surrounded by antisemitic individuals, I found myself becoming quiet, which is how I think many of us act when we are faced with systemic bigotry: Quiet. I wonder how we can challenge these moments in a way that moves us forward, without the aggression or negativity that generally accompanies such challenges.

It's important to note that people won't change unless they *want* to change; they need to be open to acceptance rather than backlashing the same negativity that drives them to be bigoted and biased. The best way we can deal with those who are fearful of change is to continue being ourselves and propelling our positive influence more loudly. Our influence can change culture, especially when we take the high road and know what is needed to move the marker in the direction of positivity. We must not get trapped in these cycles of bigotry and bias, and we should not remain quiet; we should become positively louder.

If we truly want to be a positive influence, then we must challenge ourselves to recognize the cycle that traps all of us and the tendency we have within ourselves to influence through bias and negativity toward those who are different from us. When we all begin to work on our ability to accept and include others, we get closer to understanding and creating positive cultures within our communities.

Key Takeaways: What is True Diversity?

- True diversity requires opening the discussion of diversity to include more than the mainstream topics of race, gender, and sexual orientation.
- Diversity is both how you are alike and how you are different from others, and while you may tend to gravitate toward people who are more like you, if you become too caught up in this feeling of comfort, you may fall into "us versus them" thinking.
    - An "us versus them" mentality instigates negativity, bias, and bigotry, and can lead you to an inability to accept or acknowledge those who are dissimilar.
- When you perpetuate an influence where it is acceptable to segregate based on diversity, you hurt all of humanity.
- People won't change unless they want to change. The best way to help others want to be better is by being better yourself and using your influence to help them make positive changes in their lives.
- To review different visible and invisible traits of diversity, refer to the diversity iceberg graphic in this section.

Culture

We, as individuals, live with our own culture and exude that culture through our influence. We can also live inside of several different cultures and be influenced by them. By way of definition, culture is the environment we exist in and how the individuals in that environment interact with one another. Culture is built, felt, and maintained by those who live in these environments. Our work, home, or even school cultures are probably all different in their own way. The cultures we immerse ourselves in and manifest in our daily lives can have a subtle or dramatic influence on us, depending on how open and perceptive we are to that influence.

Culture is a powerful force in all our lives, and our individual influence is constantly adding to the mix. We consciously *and* subconsciously contribute to the culture of the moment as well as the culture of the future. For example, if we are witnessing someone get bullied or talked down to, we can contribute to building a positive culture by either intervening to help alleviate the pain of the person being demeaned, or we can choose to ignore the situation and allow it to continue even though there could be negative repercussions for allowing it to happen. If we intervene or don't, we influence culture in the moment as well as the future. This is one reason our individual influence is so powerful: We can consciously create the culture we wish to see just by the actions we take and words we choose to say today. Conversely, sometimes we contribute to culture subconsciously. This stems from us simply being who we are as individuals. It's embedded in our bias, habits, character, ego, attitude, maturity, goals, and more. Just being who we are contributes to these cultures, which is why it is so important to know ourselves, understand our influence, and use it positively.

We typically construct our cultures, or we conform to others. For example, consider start-ups; due to how new they are, they have yet to develop a company culture. Company culture is made by the individuals who are part of the initial team and the policies and procedures they decide to write for the foundation of that new company. Culture stems from us as individuals, and we carry it on through our influence. On the other hand, we also conform to cultures. My travels in Asia have allowed me a decent comparison of Asian culture in Asia and Asian culture in places like Chinatown in San Francisco. From what I have seen, the culture is so close in these two places that when you are in Chinatown, you almost forget you are in an American city.

Maintaining a positive culture, or even building one, requires an immense amount of responsibility. How we communicate and compose ourselves is how we develop the culture around us. It's created by choosing to take the high road, owning our mistakes, remaining fair and objective, and all the areas covered in this series in pursuit of being a positive influence. When and if we choose to uphold our values, that adds to our individual culture and culture as a team. I say "when and if" because if we define our values and then choose not to stick to them, that does build culture, just one that will look different than what we began with. That change may or may not be positive. Build a positive culture by sticking to your word and being honest, staying true to yourself, and ensuring that even when life gets hard, you don't abandon what you believe in; unless, of course, if what you believe in was wrong for you, then it's okay to change.

One of the best ways to keep ourselves centered in who we are, in an effort to live and maintain positive culture and influence, is to slow down and listen. Listen to what others have to say, take it in, check the facts and data, have open and thoughtful discussions if you have opposing viewpoints, and remain kind and civil. When you know where the high road is, stay positive and remain consistent in who you are and stand up for what you believe in. Culture is built through consistent action.

While consistency is key, it's important not to shy away from, or fear, change. Change is meant to enhance a company and make it better overall. Change should be embraced in a way that supports the integrity of the company's culture. We must remember why the change was necessary in the first place and stay focused on where the company is headed, as well as where it's been. Culture requires consistency from the people who build it, and, unless a culture is negative, it shouldn't shift with the change program. Culture can remain the same, acting as a constant pillar while the company is elevated around it. Allow positive culture to soothe anxieties surrounded by change. Change is inevitable, but we can make it palpable by supporting and maintaining positive culture.

In the end, we all build company culture: All of us contribute to our teams. We build that culture through our influence, through the words we say and the actions we take. We can either choose to actively participate in building a positive culture, or we can stand by and allow that culture to be decided for us. However, to be positive leaders—for ourselves, our family, friends, coworkers, and strangers—we must be responsible for our influence. Being responsible for our influence means knowing ourselves fully so we can contribute what makes us each individual to that which is greater than us.

Key Takeaways: Culture

- You live inside multiple cultures; you create your internal culture, as well as operating within cultures around you (whether they be your work, community, or other spaces). You influence those cultures as much as they influence you (depending on how perceptive you are to that influence).
- Maintaining and building culture takes immense responsibility, focus, and consistency.
- Build a positive culture by sticking to your word and being honest, staying true to yourself, and ensuring that even when life gets hard, you don't abandon what you know to be true while allowing yourself to be open to learning new things.

Equality versus Equity

If you're a bit confused by the terms "equality" and "equity," I don't blame you. Equality and equity are very similar, but, like a Venn diagram, they have some distinct differences that can help you to create safe spaces for yourself, your teams, and others you may influence. Let's define these terms and start a discussion to identify their subtle differences. Please note that these are the generally agreed-upon definitions of equality and equity; however, it gets tricky when we start the discussion on applying these concepts within our spheres of influence. Equality is simple: It's treating all people in the same manner regardless of their differences. If you're the type of person to hold the door for others, it means taking the opportunity to hold the door for *all* people when you have the opportunity and not just when you feel that they deserve it.

Equity can be more challenging to describe: It's typically defined as treating people based on their individual needs and differences. This is like having handicap parking or a ramp for wheelchairs to easily access the building if the only means of getting in are stairs (and these aren't just equitable, they are the law in America). Or it's like having audio recordings in museums or art exhibits for those who experience visual impairment. It's offering different ways to read, using Braille, audio, eBooks, and even hard copies. Being equitable simply means that we recognize that some types of diversity require different needs, and we aim to offer each individual person what they need (which may not be the same as what other people require).

Not everyone needs a wheelchair and not everyone needs hearing aids; equality would be giving everyone the exact same thing, while equity looks at need. To make this difference between equality and equity as simple to understand as possible, you'll find a simple drawing of the differences between people based on height in reaching fruit from the apple tree.

EQUALITY

EQUITY

While this graphic offers an easy visual to understand the differences between equality and equity, in application, it can become pretty convoluted. Why? It really boils down to the fact that because we are all different, we all define things differently for ourselves. We define our meaning of success and prosperity individually, and we apply our means of being equal and equitable individually. This is essentially setting up rules and judging how to treat people based on how we feel inside. This might be based on our values, the values of our company, our personality, or something else entirely. The key to equality and equity is being fair, so while it is tricky to define what these things might mean at a global level, or even for someone else, defining it for ourselves should be easy. What is most important is our application of our definition, and our consistent application defines whether we treat others in an equal and equitable way.

To be equal and equitable, we must apply the rules that we define for ourselves to everyone in the same manner, regardless of our bias. One topic that is often discussed in the workplace regarding equality and equity is choosing who to give a pay raise, who to promote, and even who to mentor. For some, it's based on level of experience, education, or even potential. For others, it's based on loyalty and how long someone has been with the company. It's different on each team, but the key to being truly equal and equitable is staying consistent in our way of thinking. For example, if you choose to base pay rate on level of experience and education, everyone with the same level of experience and education performing the same job should have the same pay rate (regardless of their gender, ability, race, or any other diverse trait).

However, suppose you have an employee who experiences a physical or mental disability and requires additional tools to perform their work or a modified physical workspace. In that case, you need to provide the necessary tools so they have the opportunity to complete their work and reach their goals to the best of their abilities (the same as their non-disabled team members). Not everyone would need those additional tools or modified workspaces, and this is what is equitable about giving certain people what they need to thrive. Considering pay rate again, you wouldn't change the pay rate of those who have a physical or mental disability if you decide to base pay rate on level of education. Just because someone needs a modification in their physical space or an additional tool to assist them in performing their work, doesn't mean their pay rate should be disproportionately influenced. The point is that you need to define what is equal, and that will then help establish what equity means.

One question that comes up for us is, "Are there any reasons we could or should define our individual application of equality and equity based on what makes us diverse?" And while pondering this question over a long period, we continually came back to the same answer: No. When it comes to hiring, firing, promoting, or defining pay rate, it shouldn't be defined by what makes people diverse. For example, if you take an LGBTQ+ non-profit organization, it wouldn't be equal or equitable to only hire people who are part of this community when there are many people who aren't part of this community who consider themselves allies. While this organization would be defined by something that makes them diverse, they shouldn't apply that measurement of diversity to their hiring process.

Now, imagine that people receive different rates for the same job with the same education level, experience, or time with the team and those people find out they receive different pay rates; this scenario would make it difficult to foster inclusion as it would create animosity amongst team members and eventually destroy culture. One of the most important aspects of being equal and equitable is banishing bias, which requires that you be fair and inclusive of diversity while coming to terms with people who are like and unlike you. Without equality and equitability, inclusion is difficult to foster. And without a clear-cut approach to inclusion, diversity will be impossible to foster on any team.

Key Takeaways: Equality versus Equity

- Equality refers to treating all people in the same manner regardless of their differences.
- Equity is defined as treating people based on their individual needs and differences.
- Applying equality and equity looks different for everyone. This is essentially setting up rules and judging how to treat people based on how you feel inside. This might be based on your values, the values of your company, your personality, or something else entirely.
- The key to truly being equal and equitable is being fair and consistent in your application. You must apply the rules that you define for yourself to everyone in the same manner, regardless of your bias.

Inclusion of Diversity

While diversity can be easy to gain and prove, inclusion doesn't simply follow behind just because diversity is present. And make no mistake, if you do not have proper inclusion initiatives, diversity will not thrive on your team. Inclusion is a conscious action; it requires showing up in your everyday life with the intention to make everyone you influence feel heard, included, and like they belong in that space free of judgment for what makes them diverse.

Knowing how to treat people inclusively is a skill that needs to be developed because it's not something that inherently comes easy for everyone. Our brains are hardwired to not only seek out patterns but to make us feel as comfortable as possible by assimilating with those who appear to be like us on the surface. While there is nothing wrong with this comfort, it can trap us in an echo chamber of our biases, making it more difficult to ponder or accept conflicting information. This could result in negative influence and make others feel as if they don't belong, thus squeezing them out.

Inclusion requires us to get comfortable with feeling uncomfortable, at least at certain times when we are in a new experience. Our brains don't particularly like to be challenged, hence why it is called a "challenge"! But if we are determined to create spaces of inclusion and be a positive influence, then we must set the intention of challenging bias when it creeps up. We must ask ourselves if we are respecting others' differences or if we are oppressing them, and then think about why and how we might look at those differences in a more objective and positive manner.

We believe that our influence is our greatest responsibility. Therefore, we are all accountable for providing a foundation of inclusion in our areas of influence. Being a leader means not only talking the talk but walking the walk. Leaders must show their team through their words and actions that they are committed to fostering a culture of inclusion. Without leadership engagement, an inclusive culture will not be sustained and will become unviable. This includes setting measures of accountability for those who fail to create and build on a culture of inclusion, either by helping them learn to get out of their own way or implementing a progressive education process to provide an opportunity to learn the value and positivity of inclusion, diversity, and equity.

One way to foster inclusion is through mentorship programs. Taking new team members under your wing to demonstrate the culture of the organization through your actions is one of the best ways to ensure that your team is inclusive. You aren't above them; you are their mentor, leader, team member, and guide, regardless of what might make them different from you or others. Your organization may also consider accepting the move to share their preferred pronouns—as defined by the individual—in the workplace or developing team bonding groups. The team at IA meets once a week for something called Gratitude Group. The sole purpose of this group is to learn and share what we are grateful for. It is a group that is not divided by anything other than our wish to come together in positivity. IA also provides one-to-one mentorship that is open for everyone.

Now, let's throw a small wrench into our understanding of inclusion: Simply focusing on what makes people different isn't being inclusive, as it offers the potential to exclude them based on their differences. Additionally, ignoring what makes people diverse may also exclude them. Are you confused? On the surface, this contradictory phenomenon doesn't really make any sense. Don't focus on someone's differences… but don't ignore them? What's the key factor in this? Your actions, your words, and how you show up with your influence every single day is key to making people feel included.

We shouldn't solely focus on someone's differences because it may make them feel excluded; we all want to feel like we belong and fit in. We also shouldn't ignore differences because they represent the beauty of diversity. We can walk this line by bringing our empathy to bear. We can express that we care to know more about others' experience and life and that we value them as human beings. How has their diversity shaped their world lens, and what can we learn from it?

If we offend someone with a misguided comment or question, there's a simple solution: Apologize. Ask follow-up questions. Recognize that the person who is feeling hurt is trying to be heard. Don't provide justifications like, "I'm just kidding, don't be so emotional/sensitive." This is invalidating and assumptive, which we don't have the right to do. Everyone lives in their own reality, and we can see this situation as an opportunity to step closer to the issue; choose curiosity over judgment. No matter what comes out of the conversation, we *will* walk away being that much more aware of the world around us. We can then influence ourselves and others with a more positive approach when these issues arise.

These are just some ways we can embrace the challenges of diversity and inclusion, rather than shying away from it. If you want to find more ways, call a team meeting and have a brainstorming session with everyone. However, it's important to note that this will only work if your organization has a foundation of trust established; otherwise, team members may feel unable to speak up without fear of retribution or perhaps even embarrassment.

Key Takeaways: Inclusion of Diversity

- While diversity may seem easy to gain, inclusion doesn't simply follow behind. If you do not have proper inclusion initiatives, diversity will not thrive.
- Inclusion is a conscious action; it requires showing up in your everyday life with the intention to make everyone you influence feel heard, included, and like they belong.
- Mentor new or minority team members to help foster cultures of inclusion. Or develop team bonding groups, like IA's Gratitude Group.
- Don't define individuals by their differences, but don't ignore their differences either.
- If you say something that is taken negatively, apologize. After identifying that it wasn't your intent to cause discomfort or to alienate, ask follow-up questions to learn more and understand what went wrong.

Battling Bias

If you read *Individual Influence*, you will remember our discussion on the topic of subconscious and unconscious bias. Here, we'll take it a step further. In order to be a positive influence on your teams, you need to understand how to battle both the bias you find in yourself *and* the bias you see in others. Identifying and understanding bias is important because, most of the time, the bias is not true, yet it impacts your thoughts and actions if you choose not to confront it. When you judge someone based on their outside appearance before you get to know who they are internally, you are generalizing them through your biases.

Remember, everyone is a unique individual and deserves to be treated with respect. To quickly recap, the best way to uncover and get over bias is to start seeking your biases out. Look for the blind spots in your thinking, question snap judgments about others (even the good ones), and have compassion for yourself on this journey. Your interpretations of the world might not be wrong, but they might not be right either; that's okay. Nobody is perfect, so when you work to identify your bias, you must remain curious and omit justification. Ask others to be honest if they identify bias in your way of thinking and be open to exploring that. While it may not feel good to be challenged, slow down, take a deep breath, show yourself some love and empathy, and give yourself permission to learn more about the world. Expanding your mind with new information can only bring good things.

You may find that someday someone identifies what they believe is a bias within you and they fail to see the intent behind your words or actions. Intent is hard to measure and prove; stating your intent requires trust, as there are some people who will use intent as a justification to brush something off rather than being transparent about their true intent. For example, there are some who might find the term "colorblind" to be racist, signaling that those who use this term fail to recognize the differences and life experiences of people of color. For others, the intent behind this word is to state that they simply see human beings and do not judge them by the color of their skin, which is the opposite of racism. In this situation, trust with others helps to pave the way for better communication, with fewer misunderstandings.

Even in situations where people who use terms like "colorblind" have positive intent, there are always some who will follow along with the crowd without truly understanding what it means. The ignorance of these people begins to cast a shadow on something that should be positive. Ignorance isn't inherently bad, but it can cause negativity (perhaps unconsciously) when we spew words or take actions simply to follow the crowd rather than knowing and understanding. We cannot measure intent because we will always face the puzzle of perception, and through this, we will find difficulty in pleasing everyone. Through understanding that we are all diverse, we understand that our different life experiences lead us to have various responses and emotions to stimuli. Some may feel no response while others may feel completely set off.

If we are faced with a moment when someone challenges us by identifying a possible bias, there are a lot of things we must consider. In the moment, we should behave respectfully and gather more information to gain insight into how they came to this conclusion from their perspective. We might learn something, but we might find that we disagree if it's an issue of intent or objectivity. Like we mentioned earlier, we can't please everyone. We may find that some people are not bothered by our behavior at all, while others are offended. This is just part of diversity; no two people (no matter how similar they may seem) will think or act alike. By being true to ourselves and battling our bias, we can suit the influence we wish to be.

Once a bias is identified, one of the best and only ways to uproot this bias is to continually be on the lookout for that bias and to challenge it when it arises. The only way to change is to set our intention for removing bias and being diligent in challenging it. The more we do this (much like creating a new habit), the easier it will become. In addition, the more we challenge ourselves to disprove our biases, the smaller the bias will become (meaning, the less frequently it will pop up). When we decide to challenge and overcome our bias, we may find that, someday, our bias does not come up anymore. However, if we fail to challenge and overcome our identified bias, it will be easy to justify why we have that bias. Unfortunately, justification of our bias will only make that bias more prevalent and ingrained in our way of thinking.

Justification

It's easy to dismiss and justify our bias because that's easier than challenging and overcoming it. Our perception of life, the opinions we make along the way, who we are, and the experiences we have all create the biases we hold. As humans, we often tend to take the easiest and simplest way out of things, which is why we tend to justify our biases, actions, words, and more. We may find that, at times, we come up with justifications when we know we are doing something negative, against our values, or that we do not approve of. Justifications offer us an easy way out because they allow us to dismiss whatever thoughts are making us uncomfortable.

Justification can act as trap that allows us to abandon our values because it offers us relief from what we know is wrong. For example, even for those of us who value honesty, we all lie to some degree every day; some of them are white lies, and some of them are big webs of lies. However, someone who outwardly values honesty, for instance, can be caught in the trap of justification when they are put in a position where they either lie or feel like they need to lie. Justification is how we can have conditions surrounding our values.

Bias is very similar in that we tend to justify the biases we or others identify within us because it makes us uncomfortable to admit that we are wrong, to challenge ourselves to align with our values, or to grow as individuals. We are more comfortable when we can justify our words or actions because, again, it allows us to dismiss those feelings of discomfort. Therefore, we must learn to identify when we are using justification to absolve ourselves and how this might affect us and/or others. While escaping this justification and bias may be tricky at times, in order to become our most positive influence, it is imperative that we set intentions for identifying and overcoming not only our bias but our *justifications* for our bias.

One way to challenge our justifications is to allow ourselves to assume that we are wrong. Typically, justifications occur because we assume we are in the right, which leads us to take the easy path of not challenging ourselves. However, if we assume we are wrong (which might not be the case, but it's a good exercise to start with), we can begin to construct theories of why we might be wrong. If we can disprove these theories, perhaps we are right; however, we might find theories to disprove our justification and bias to shed light on the answers we need to move forward with acceptance. By challenging ourselves through assuming that we could be wrong, we aid our ability to keep an open mind and view the situation from different perspectives. Just as we must work on uprooting our bias and justifications, we must work on our ability to assume we might be wrong.

Mary shared a good example of this process of bias, justification, and taking the stance that she was wrong in *Individual Influence.* To recap that story, Mary had a professor point out a generational bias, which she immediately dismissed (justification). However, over the course of a few days, she wondered if it was possible that she did have a generational bias (by assuming her justification could be wrong) and began a process of self-reflection to identify if the bias could be true. She concluded that it was true, even though having such a bias went against her core values (as many biases do). This process can be uncomfortable, but it can also be immensely helpful.

Bias must be addressed if we are to grow into our most positive influence. It doesn't mean we will be perfect or that we will come to a point in our lives when we have uprooted all bias; to be biased is to be human. This is a truth we must accept while we are on this journey, as it will help us have compassion for ourselves and others. This process is about continual growth, not a final destination. There are instances where justifying our bias won't hurt anyone but us, but at what cost? We risk damaging our influence and becoming set in the ways of justification. To justify and continue the habit is easy; to break the habit and start a new pattern of thinking takes time and dedication, but it gets easier and is worth the effort. Be honest about why we justify or why we don't challenge ourselves to be better. Justification gives us nothing except false peace of mind. It is only through challenging and being transparent with ourselves that we will be able to overcome our bias, identify its root cause, and move forward with presence in our ways of thinking, speaking, and doing.

Key Takeaways: Battling Bias

- When you judge someone based on their external attributes before you get to know who they are internally, you are generalizing about them through your biases.
- Intent is hard to measure and prove; there are some people who will use intent as a justification to brush something off rather than being transparent about true intent.
- Once a bias is identified, one of the best (and only) ways to uproot it is to continually be on the lookout for that bias and to challenge it when it arises.
- Justification will only make bias more prevalent and ingrained in your way of thinking.
- Your perception of life, the opinions you make along the way, who you are, and the experiences you have all create the biases you hold.
- Justification allows you a way to dismiss uncomfortable feelings associated with being challenged.
- One way to challenge your justification is to assume you are wrong and consider theories to support why you might be wrong.
- The entire process of battling your bias and challenging justification is about continual growth rather than a final destination.

Diversity, Equity, and Inclusion Reflection

When considering the roles of diversity, equity, inclusion, bias, and culture in your life, keep your mind open to the vastness of these topics. True diversity is so broad, it could be difficult to comprehend, while equity can be defined individually but should be applied equally from one source. Inclusion must be wielded mindfully and without judgment, even in moments where you don't perfectly apply it. Bias can be invasive when justified repeatedly if you do not uproot it consciously, and lastly, culture is something you can shape and change with your influence. Remind yourself that you are a human being who is driven by the desire to feel happy and like you belong, which is something you share with the rest of humanity. This reminder may help you in moving forward with the ability to be your best influence while remembering the importance and beauty of diversity.

Concluding Thoughts

As I am left gathering my last thoughts for you, I am filled with excitement and positivity. If you learn nothing else, my hope is that you have learned that you are influential. You don't have to be famous or have a large following on social media to be an integral part of this life, because we are all important. Your influence spans many lives and grows with each day. You are important, and through that importance, it is imperative that you be your best self.

I am reminded of a quote by Dr. Seuss:

"Today you are you, that is truer than true. There is no one alive who is you-er than you."[6]

You owe it to yourself to be a positive influence, to see what you can do and who you can be as a positive leader. Your greatest responsibility is your individual influence. Take it upon yourself to BE the best influence you can be.

6. Dr. Seuss, *Happy Birthday to You!* 2005, HarperCollins Children's Books

Join Our Team

Are you ready to join the "'I' in Team" series team? Stay up to date on all things related to positive influence, leadership development, management, building teams, and more when you follow us on social media!

Facebook: The "I" in Team Series
LinkedIn: The "I" in Team Series
Twitter: @IinTeamSeries
Instagram: @theiinteamseries
YouTube: The "I" in Team Series (watch our vlogcast)
Website: www.IABusinessAdvisors.com/the-i-in-team-series

For more information on the work IA Business Advisors does for our clients, please follow us on social media and visit our website! Reach out to us. We would love to help you and your team grow and thrive.

Facebook: IA Business Advisors
LinkedIn: IA Business Advisors
Twitter: @IA_Biz_Advisors
Instagram: @ia_businessadvisors
YouTube: IA Business Advisors
Website: www.IABusinessAdvisors.com

Thank you, and welcome to our team!